Courtesy Arizona State Museum   Photo: James W. Manson, n.d.

IN MUSIC, NECESSITY IS THE MOTHER OF INVENTION.

THE LAST OF THE
S E R I S

PISCHEL YEARBOOKS, INC.
P. O. Box 36, Marceline, Missouri 64658

THE LAST OF THE
SERIS

By DANE COOLIDGE *and*
MARY ROBERTS COOLIDGE

WITH PHOTOGRAPHS BY
DANE COOLIDGE

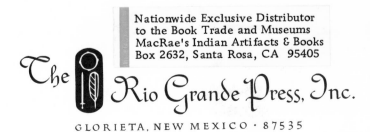

Nationwide Exclusive Distributor
to the Book Trade and Museums
MacRae's Indian Artifacts & Books
Box 2632, Santa Rosa, CA 95405

The Rio Grande Press, Inc.

GLORIETA, NEW MEXICO · 87535

1971
© The Rio Grande Press, Inc.,
Glorieta, N.M. 87535

First edition from which this edition
was reproduced was supplied by
MRS. NANCY ROBERTS COLLINS
Menlo Park, California 94025

A RIO GRANDE CLASSIC
First published in 1939

LIBRARY OF CONGRESS CARD CATALOG
71-153199

I.S.B.N. 87380-078-8

First Printing 1971

The Rio Grande Press, Inc.
GLORIETA, NEW MEXICO · 87535

Publisher's Preface

Chance took us to Kino Bay, Sonora, on the west coast of mainland Mexico. In October 1970, partner John Strachan, friend Edward J. Ruda and his sister Elizabeth of Danville, Ill., and I went to Hermosillo on business. While there, it occurred to us to drive over to *Bahía Kino* just sightseeing--an easy trip of some 70 miles over a good blacktop road.

So we went, and we're happy that we did. Old Kino Bay village is pretty much as it always has been, but what struck us dumb was New Kino Bay village. From Hermosillo, Mexican Highway No. 16 comes into New Kino Bay village around a sweeping curve, and there, before our delighted eyes, was a breathtaking panorama of limpid, sparkling sea, an island upthrust like some proud sailing ship, a glistening white beach that curved out of sight to the north, and a road ahead of us that followed the beach to a rocky headland looming distantly on the horizon.

But it was the motel that caught and held our astonished eyes. To the right, on a rise that commanded an unobstructed view in all directions, sat the lavish *Posada del Mar*. In a stark and sere desert setting, this luxurious establishment looked more like a movie set than a commercial enterprise. It was beautiful, even magnificent; such a motel in the United States would be far out of our modest price range.

We ogled the vivid green terraces, the balustraded stone stairways, the formal gardens, the wrought iron ornaments, the glistening pool patio with the colorful umbrellas. The elegant restaurant caught our eye as we passed, alongside the road in its own splendid setting. Without even asking, we figured we couldn't afford it.

We drove down the curving avenida towards the dead end at *Restaurante Caverna del Seri.* There we strolled up to the diner's patio, then down to where the surf softly caressed the sandy shore, and where the soaring stone headland thrust its powerful feet into the waves. The offshore breeze was soft upon our cheeks; to the nostrils, it smelled of salt and marine life. We learned that the island in the south distance, across from *Posada del Mar,* was *Isla Alcatraz* –in English, Pelican Island.

Off to the east from our viewpoint, lay the brown, dry hills of the *Desierto Sonora,* counterpointed with marching ranks of the majestic *cacteas Saguaro.* The vigorous growth of dry country vegetation hid the harsh clay soil. Overhead the sky was a brilliant azure, spun over with a skein of clouds and molten with golden sunshine. It was lovely.

We noticed two other motels on the way back down the curving *avenida.* One was the Motel Kino Bay, with 24 units and a 120-trailer park. We ate subsequently at their little restaurant (the food was very good) several times, as we did at *Restaurante Caverna del Seri.* If the *Motel Posada Santa Gamma,* further south on the seashore side of the *avenida,* has a restaurant we didn't see it. The "no vacancy" sign was out on both motels, so for us it was either return to Hermosillo after dark or try *Posada del Mar.*

It was a blue-eyed gringo behind the registration desk in the elegant lobby. And, yes, to our surprise, we could afford to stay there. We were actually astonished at the rates and the accommodations; we rarely have stayed in quarters quite so nice, and never so inexpensively. Nor have we ever encountered such a warm hospitality on the part of a motel manager. The blue-eyed gringo was Mr. Bud Hender, a citizen of the United States as well as the Republic of Mexico. He and Mrs. Hender did everything for us but turn out the lights at bedtime, meanwhile entertaining us as duties permitted with tales of Seriland. In Hermosillo, we subsequently met Mr. Hender's business colleague, Señor Santiago Garcia de la Garza, who was as hospitable and friendly as Mr. Hender.

The next day, at breakfast in the dining room *(LaLoma Blanca),* our waiter–doubling as a guide–offered to take us to *Chueca* village of the Seri Indians, some 18 or 20 miles up the coast from *Bahia Kino.* We naturally said yes. His name was Sergio Gonzales, from Guaymas; we found him a real jewel. It developed he could speak Seri as well as English, altho he later told us the Indians were speaking to him a sort of pidgin-Spanish, and not a Seri language.

We drove up to *Chueca* that afternoon, over a road meant obviously only for tanks or jeeps–certainly it was no road for a low-slung station wagon. Still, we made it. We drove into *Chueca* and the land that time forgot.

From all directions came the Seri Indians towards us, each handling and constantly polishing with a rag one of his or her lovely ironwood carvings. We had, in our bibliographic studies and research, often encountered references to the Seri Indians, but here we were suddenly face to face with them. Our surprise was boundless.

First and foremost, the adults were a singularly handsome people. Secondly, they were good natured and always laughing or smiling. Thirdly, what they offered to sell us was their gleaming, marvelous carvings. Here we encountered a people scarcely emerged fully from the Stone Age, yet handicrafting objects of art that for sophistication, for grace, for purity of line and symmetry, could hardly be surpassed. Indeed, we think no civilized artist could duplicate the work of these aboriginal people. Upon all sides we were pressed to examine the objects; tugs and pulls on our sleeves, clothing and hips from all around revealed an astounding collection of superb, stylized reproductions of marine and desert creatures. We were overwhelmed completely by these beautiful works of art and their strange creators—here an owl, there a shark, a porpoise, yonder a whale or a seal, now a seal or a turtle or a sheep or a manta ray; it was nearly impossible to determine which piece was the more beautiful, so we bought them all that day.

We are hard put to describe the Seri Indians and do it gently or gracefully. They wore the clothing of the white man, but always it had been worn too long and too steadily. Personal hygiene was nowhere visible or suspected. Their village of *Chueca* must be seen to be believed, for it is a ghetto of shocking proportions. Still, as the women walked, they strode erect and proud, unabashedly free of such non-essentials as brassieres. The men were lithe and strong, and very quick as they moved about. The teeth of all of them, universally revealed in their constant smiling and laughing were worn to red stumps. Sergio said this was because of the hardness of the water they drank, but we think more likely it was because of the sand and grit that must be ubiquitous in their food. Still, their brown eyes danced and sparkled, the women were shy and the men were modest. It was, for us, a strange but delightful contact—altho Edward's sister Elizabeth was ready to leave almost before we stopped the car.

And the children! Oh, those kids! Some were bare all over, some wore remnants of cloth that once might have been planned garments. With a gulf full of warm water (albeit salty), the shy but active youngsters presumably never went near it. Their hair was unconfined, each strand seeking its own destiny outward; it was not "teased", as American women use the term, but it was surely tormented. As the hair hung down untrimmed and unbraided, it covered the brown eyes of most of them, inducing Edward to remark that it surely gave them a dark outlook on life.

In the midst of our visit, we were unsettled utterly to suddenly look down into the smiling face of a five year old–a freckled face with a skin as fair as the dawn, with light straight hair that could have come from Norway, with eyes as green as the depths of the gulf of California. He was a beautiful boy, perfectly at home with his *compadres.*

Chueca? In the years gone by, we later learned, the Seri Indians had lived in *jacales*–shelters not even huts, made of brush and desert growth over a framework of stakes. There were no *jacales* visible in *Chueca* when we were there. What we saw were ramshackle aggregations of junk salvaged from the flotsam and jetsam of the sea, and from the trash dumps of New and Old Kino villages and perhaps even from the dumps of Hermosillo. The Indians travel far and wide, barefoot, very swiftly, over the coarse and rough and harsh miles of the desert.

It was anomalous to see these rude and primitive shelters alongside a stack of Coca-Cola cases half filled with empty bottles. It came as a bit unsettling to see empty Folger and Maxwell House coffee tins, 50 gallon Oscar Meyer lard drums and every imaginable kind of plastic wrap, sheet and container. . .the rubbish of a social order beyond the grasp of the Seri Indians, but items which they often found desirable or useful to themselves.

Like most Indians, the Seris refused to allow pictures of either themselves, or their village. At the sight of our camera, the friendliness on every face turned troubled or hostile; we put the camera away, and all was immediately well--at least on the surface. Sergio could communicate with the Seris, and did--to their tremendous pleasure. It was obvious he was a frequent and welcome visitor. He was a particular favorite of the women, and small wonder, since he is a most attractive man.

While perhaps we could have walked around and in- spected the village, we were uncertain if that was the thing to do and Sergio said it most definitely was not. We could see no great merit in the mere satisfaction of our vulgar curiosity, so we got back in the car to leave. Partner John found a sack of apples we had not eaten, and began to pass them out as we drove away. The children and adults both ran alongside with hands out until there were no more. We did not see how they could eat the fruit--particularly apples--with the stumps that served as teeth, but in moments we were around the bend and out of sight of *Chueca* and the Indians.

Mr. and Mrs. Hender, at *Posada del Mar,* could tell us little about the Seri people and neither could Sergio. We soon had a crowd about us, though, motel guests and transient tourists admiring the sleek ironwood carvings. Everybody wanted one. As we were to later discover, the carvings are immensely popular to the cognoscenti in Arizona and California; they are almost living legends in their own time. From a gringo trader or store in the States, the carvings are rare and expensive, and justifiably so.

The Seri Indians were not making the ironwood carvings in the days when Dane and Mary Coolidge were at Kino Bay, so we are not including much about them here. We are including a few pictures of fine pieces in the photo folio at the back of the book, but a detailed account of the origin and development of this handicraft is left for the McGee volume. There the interested reader can find the story of the carvings, and a gallery of splendid color pictures of fine pieces. In passing, we might mention that the first edition BAE Report had only four color plates. We have added many more, of the Indians, their carvings and their village at Desemboque.

We returned to Glorieta and went about our business as one always does after being away for awhile. We began to research the Seri Indians, only to discover there was really not much in print about them. The Arizona State Museum recently published a handsome four-color brochure, with many pictures, which it sells at the souvenir counter in the Museum. We suddenly discovered, almost by accident, a first edition of this book--*The Last of the Seris*. We bought it at once, and of course, decided immediately to reprint it. We also discovered that Anthropologist W.J. McGee had written a paper entitled *The Seri Indians* in the BAE Annual Report, 1895-1896. We procured a copy from T.N. Luther, rare book dealer in Shawnee Mission, Kans., and decided to reprint that, also.

In checking with the Library of Congress Copyright Office, we found that the copyright for *The Last of the Seris* had been properly renewed and it would be necessary for us to locate the heirs of authors Dane and Mary Coolidge. With the help of the Copyright Office, and others, we finally located Mrs. Nancy Roberts Collins, present holder of the copyright, and a niece of the late Mary Roberts Coolidge. Almost at the same time, we were fortunate to locate Mr. Coit Coolidge, a nephew of the late Dane Coolidge. Both people responded cordially and favorably to our request for permission to reprint *The Last of the Seris;* we thank them both for their gracious and friendly cooperation.

Mrs. Collins sent us some photographs of the two authors, as did Mr. Coolidge (who at present is Project Coordinator of the North State Cooperative Library System in Chico, Calif.). Later, he also wrote for us a Memoriam to Dane and Mary, which follows these pages. We consider it a touching and poignant tribute to a warm and memorable relationship. We are most grateful to Mr. Coit Coolidge for taking the time to prepare this for us.

Dane Coolidge was born in Natick, Mass., on March 24, 1873. He attended Stanford University to complete his education, thereafter becoming a collector of live animals, birds and reptiles for famous and prestigious institutions. On July 30, 1906, at the age of 33, he met and married Mary Roberts--a second marriage for her and a first for him. Together they became the focus of a most select and exclusive literary circle, living graciously and well from the royalties of his many writings. He died August 8, 1940, at their home called Dwight Way End in Berkeley, Calif.

Mary Roberts (nee Elizabeth Burroughs) was an esteemed and noted writer in her own right when she married Dane. She was born at Kingsbury, Ind., October 28, 1860. She took a bachelor's and a master's degree at Cornell University, and a Ph.D. at Stanford. She was, thereafter, deeply involved in sociological work and studies. Like Dane, she was a prolific writer. Most of her work arose from her interest in the Indians of the Southwest, probably her best being *The Rainmakers*. She died also at Dwight Way End, April 13, 1945.

The Last of the Seris was published in 1939, although material for it was obtained in 1930. While we are not professional anthropologists, we thought we could obtain some information and photographs of the Seri Indians as they are today, and we have done so. After our visit in October, we returned to Kino Bay and Seriland in February, 1971, for more photographs and information, hoping to add a bit of up-to-date data in the McGee paper. In a hazardous but exciting trip (of 70 miles one way) through the desert to Desemboque, we were able to photograph long range some pictures we could not otherwise have obtained.

At the same time, thanks to Dr. Raymond H. Thompson (head of the Anthropology Department of the University of Arizona as well as Director of the Arizona State Museum), we procured from the latter's extensive collection a selection of fine photographs of mostly posed Seri Indians, in fresh clothing. We are incorporating some of these new photographs in a folio at the back of this book. Others,and more of them, are incorporated as a folio into our reprint of the BAE McGee title.

With our emendations here, we have tried pretty much to keep the focus of our remarks on the Seri Indians at *Chueca* village–now, apparently nearly *en toto,* at Kino Bay itself. They have, with no effort at all, created a new ghetto in the desert only yards east of *Restaurante Caverna del Seri.* When we went to visit them in February 1971, now at Kino Bay, some of the adults and nearly all of the children threw rocks at us when they saw our camera. We have more to say about this adventure in our Publisher's Preface to the McGee book. We think that if you find *The Last of the Seris* interesting, you will also want to read *The Seri Indians.*

According to Mr. Hender, Mexican officials now estimate the Seri population to be some 350 Indians. Neither he nor we set this forth as a fact. Some are coming along in new generations, obviously. But whether for much longer they will retain their racial identity is a question we cannot answer. Whatever the future may hold, the relatively few individuals remaining are what is left of one of the most interesting (and historically the most savage) groups of people in Mexico.

We are delighted to republish this fine book; it is the 74th beautiful Rio Grande Classic. We will go back to *Bahia Kino* again, and probably again, and still again, for not only do we find the Seris an intensely fascinating people, we appreciate and enjoy the luxury of *Posada del Mar* and the pleasant hospitality of Bud and Mrs. Hender, and of Señor Santiago Garcia de la Garza.

Robert B. McCoy

La Casa Escuela
Glorieta, N.M., 87535
October 1971

FREDERICK J. DOCKSTADER

DIRECTOR

December 10, 1971

Mr. Robert B. McCoy, President
The Rio Grande Press, Inc.
Glorieta, New Mexico 87535

Dear Mr. McCoy:

I was most interested in your letter of November 28th
reporting your intention to proceed with the Seri Book.
Although I never knew Mary Coolidge, I was acquainted
with Dane, and we have the Coolidge Collection here at
the Museum.

Long well-known for their writings on the Indians of
the Southwest, Dane and Mary Coolidge went to Seri
country in 1932 to see for themselves just what the land
and the people were like. Lured by honest curiosity, as
they frankly admit, together with the writings of W. J.
McGee, they furthered their interest through discussions
with Alfred L. Kroeber, a leading scholar of the period.
A generation of readers had grown up with their works on
the Southwest, most notably *The Rainmakers* (1929), and
The Navajo Indians (1930), which provided an introduction
to the Hopi, Zuni and Navajo Indians. Admittedly popular
accounts, these nevertheless performed an important
function, for they were sympathetic treatments which
abandoned sensational treatment for a relatively straight-
forward account of the Native American, albeit in romantic
vein.

In the present book, the Coolidges continue this approach, as is apparent from the title; yet this remains one of the very few accounts of Seri life by non-professional anthropologists. It is a simple introduction to a little-known tribe, and the photographs, though of snapshot quality, are clear and unstaged. It is, in brief, an uncomplicated, visually honest picture of a fascinating Indian tribe.

This is a book which can be recommended to any reader, for the non-anthropologist will learn a great deal from it; and the professional scholar, unless he has lived with the Seri, will likewise profit greatly. The most remarkable quality included in the book are the drawings which are reproduced in half-tone. This is an area rarely encountered in books about Indians, and one might wish there were even more of these intriguing sketches.

The Coolidge Collection, now in the Museum of the American Indian, represents the culture of the Seri at the time of this visit, and reflects a rapid acculturation even then well under way.

The most serious negative criticism one might make of the book is the condescending tone throughout. In today's terms, this is particularly unfortunate, although in terms of the original writing, it was probably unavoidable. Such an attitude cannot be excused, yet it should also be pointed out that writings on tribes like the Seri are rare, for these people are usually overlooked in the search for more glamorous pictures of The Noble Savage. All tribes in the New World are part of the picture of the original American, and this book adds measurably to the knowledge we have of the Seri.

Most cordially yours,

Frederick J. Dockstader
Director

FJD:lmp

Memoriam

Dane and Mary Coolidge were married in 1906, a second marriage for her and a first one for him. They built the little house at the end of Dwight Way in Berkeley, California, soon after, and moved in in 1907 – they always claimed to have been refugees from the San Francisco earthquake and fire. Dane Coolidge produced many novels there, an unknown number of novelettes, and three or four books of non-fiction on western themes. It was many years later, toward the end of his career, that *The Last of the Seris* was written, and it was from this house that they planned and carried out their expedition to Kino Bay.

They had no children, and as a nephew I inherited a warm place in their hearts. Many years ago, when I was a student, they were very kind to me, often inviting me for visits and occasionally to dinner parties involving their literary friends.

In the 1920's they were at the height of their careers – Dane a novelist photographer, and Mary, Professor of Sociology at Mills College in Oakland. Their home at the end of Dwight Way was the highest house on the hill. It looked out over a vast panorama that included the East Bay communities, the whole of San Francisco Bay, and far on out to sea. The household at that time consisted of Dane and Mary, her father, a retired professor of agriculture from Cornell, and a large tabby cat named

Kitty. Kitty was very much a member of the family, but he greatly mistrusted strangers. Many a distinguished guest came and went without the slightest idea that his arrival and departure had been the object of an intense suspicion, and that his every move on the place had been scrutinized by Kitty from his secret hiding place in the Wisteria vine over the front door. At night Kitty also hunted squirrels up the hill, and, after a successful venture, often left a portion of uneaten squirrel on the rug in front of the fireplace – no doubt Kitty's idea of contributing a share toward the support of the family.

The modest frame house, covered with brown stucco, was perched high on a steep slope. It stood in the center of a rectangular plot which may have contained a couple of acres -- the boundary was marked by an acacia hedge. Father Roberts and Dane disagreed on how to develop the garden, and the upshot was an imaginary up-and-down line through the middle, scrupulously observed by both parties. On one side, Father Roberts developed his practical ideas according to the best methods of agriculture as once applied in New York State, and on the other, Dane raised masses of flowers. The hill was so steep they both had to terrace their gardens. Father Roberts built more or less cubical terraces (edged with wood). In the middle of each was a fruit tree that produced fresh fruit for the table. Farther up the hill was a small woodlot which he planted to Eucalyptus trees. In my time these were well-grown and yielded fuel for the fireplace and wood for Father Roberts' extensive trail building operations farther up the hill.

Dane, however, developed his terraces in an entirely different manner. His became long sweeping curves that followed the contour of the hill. Each terrace was three or four feet wide, and looked like a path. Here he raised masses of China lilies and many different kinds of iris.

Life at Dwight Way End, as the place was called, followed a well-organized pattern that rarely varied. Nine months of the year (the working season) Dane wrote and gardened, while Mary taught at Mills College. The other three months they took long trips together to remote places in the west and southwest, camping on cattle ranches, taking thousands of photos with a big Graflex camera, and gathering materials for Dane's books. On these trips they sought to conceal the fact that he was a writer for fear the cowboys would fill them up with tall tales. He always posed as a wandering photographer accompanied by his wife. Toward the end of his career, however, he made a project of collecting the life histories of pioneers. A few of these went into his books, but when he died in 1940, he had more than one hundred and twenty-seven in manuscript form.

During the nine months of "working time" in Berkeley, the daily routine was something like this: Mary got up early, made a fire in the fireplace, prepared breakfast in a very modern electrified kitchen, and went on to Mills College. Dane would get up about eight, and after breakfast would go to the garden, where he worked until lunch time in a leisurely way, always turning over in his imagination the seeds of the story he was writing. After lunch he retired to a small room in back of the bedroom furnished with a small mahogany desk, pigeon-holes for manuscripts, and three or four shelves for books. There he would write on a typewriter until supper time. Mary would reappear from Mills, produce a well-planned and excellently cooked dinner served about six. Dinner guests once or twice a week in the winter time were the general rule, and after dinner everyone would sit around the big wood fire in the fireplace to talk or tell stories.

In time, Dane would clear up the table, wash and dry the dishes, and put everything away. Between 8:00 and 8:30 he would quietly vanish to his writing room and work there until toward eleven o'clock. Day in and day out on working days – good days and bad days – he wrote until he had 2,000 words on paper. The work of the bad days was often scrapped, or carefully rewritten, but no matter what kind of a day it was, he turned out 2,000 words every day before quitting.

In this manner he produced more than 40 novels, and his wife helped to educate an unknown number of Mills College girls. Dane and Mary Coolidge were very close to each other in spirit and in purpose; theirs was an idyllic relationship that lasted until he died Aug. 8, 1940. *The Last of the Seris* was the last of their books.

Coit Coolidge

Chico, Calif.
November, 1971

Dane and Mary Roberts Coolidge
August 1, 1940, eight days
before Mr. Coolidge died.

Kino Bay at sunset. Tiburon Island far in the distance and a Seri
Canoe coming home.

(Photograph by Dane Coolidge)

THE LAST OF THE
SERIS

By DANE COOLIDGE and
MARY ROBERTS COOLIDGE

WITH PHOTOGRAPHS BY
DANE COOLIDGE

E. P. DUTTON & CO., INC.

NEW YORK   PUBLISHERS

CONTENTS

5

6 CONTENTS

ILLUSTRATIONS

SERI LOVE SONG

The Arrow Sings to the Bow

I am alone.
If we were married
We would go out early.
We would kill a deer.

INTRODUCTION

THERE is an island off the coast of Sonora which rises like the tip of a lost continent, saving from extinction a people from an earlier world, the Seri Indians. They are savages now but in the old days they had poets who sang songs to every fish in the sea, and to every bird and animal. Strange white men, with blue eyes and yellow hair, they say, landed on their shores and taught them how to live. Priests came, bringing a religion not unlike that of the ancient Greeks. But that was long ago and now they have relapsed into barbarism.

First of these strangers that the sea brought in was one they now call Old Wise Woman. But then she was young and beautiful, wearing long skirts like an Oriental dancer, and she gave them this song to Tiburon.

The Island Sings

Watch me dance!
I am heavy but I can dance.
See the edge of my skirt
Wave back and forth.

It is the waves of the sea
On my beach.

Of all the hundred songs sung by Santo Blanco, the medicine man, this was the only one held sacred. He sang three stanzas, but would not sing the fourth.

11

That is the Indian's way of escaping the anger of the gods—not quite to finish a song. He saw that we admired its imagery and at last, after deep thought, he said:

"All the trees and plants and flowers know this song, but I have forgotten it. I will talk with God tonight and maybe he will tell me."

He was a true pantheist, whose world was peopled with gods. For him the Old Wise Woman still dwelt on high Tiburon and flew through the air at night to see what the Seris were doing. We never got the rest of the song but in its place we received an insight into the mind of a primitive savage and heard many stories of gods and men. To gather as many songs and stories as we did we had to break through the ancient reticence of the tribe and, placating the hostile war chiefs, write down what we could, day by day. All the old songs, all the best ones, came from this one man who had learned to talk with God.

For twenty years we had been visiting the Indians of Arizona and New Mexico, particularly the Navajos, and studying their ways of living. But the reports on the primitive Seris, as given by W. J. McGee of the Bureau of Ethnology and Dr. A. L. Kroeber, of the University of California, drew us irresistibly to Kino Bay; and when we camped there in the sand dunes we found most of the tribe living in brush shelters along the beach.

After hiring the old war chiefs to get rid of them, for they knew practically nothing of the tribal mythology and ritual, we spent six weeks talking with Santo Blanco and learning their poetry and religion. He alone of this declining race remembered the stories of the old days, when yellow-haired men came among them and were received and worshiped like gods. And on the very last day he told us of the Came From Afar Men—the strange whalers who cooked whale meat in an enormous iron pot, ate it and drank the oil.

It happened so long ago that it had passed into mythology; but here is the song of the White Giants.

> Far off on the sea a whale spouts.
> The giants follow him in their boat.
> The whale goes deep to the bottom.
> They spear him in the head
> And the sea is red with blood.

It is a record of the old Norsemen who visited the west coast of Mexico long before the Spanish came. He sang it reluctantly, three verses, and could not remember the fourth. For a brief moment we had been privileged to look behind the veil which separated his world from ours. Then he remembered the gods on Tiburon and let the curtain fall.

The story of our expedition has been set down in narrative form instead of the language of a formal report; the human side of our research appealing to the sociologist, the myth and poetry to the story writer. The songs were an unexpected discovery. Revealing as they do a rare perception of the beauties of Nature, they have been transcribed word for word, without detracting from their charm by an attempt to improve the form. This exactitude we owe in great measure to our scholarly interpreter, "El Americano," whose wide experience with Indians in Spanish-American countries reduced the liability of error to a minimum.

The Indian paintings which accompany the text are

a wonderful example of Stone Age art. Santo Blanco's first picture was made with his finger in the sand, but when we supplied him with paper his enthusiasm for the new medium knew no bounds. With the black pigment which he used to mark his arrow-shafts he dashed off picture after picture; although, as far as we could learn, neither he nor any of his people had ever made paper-pictures before.

Until the day we left he was still making them; while his wife and daughters, whose only canvas had been their own faces, joined in a mad saturnalia of Art. Surely Indians as gifted as these cannot always have been savages. Their songs, their stories, their gods like those of the ancient Greeks, all point to a day when the Seris were a great people, before the White Men came.

THE LAST OF THE

S E R I S

CHAPTER I

Wild Indians

TIBURON is a rocky island in the Gulf of California, off the coast of the worst desert in North America. Otherwise the Seri Indians would long since have been exterminated, wiped out by Mexican soldiers. It is barren and mountainous and covered with cactus, with only one permanent spring; and, between it and the mainland, there flows a shark-infested channel called *El Infiernillo*—Little Hell.

When soldiers landed to kill them, the Seris fled to caves where ollas of water had been buried, and hid till they went away. And, since men and horses must drink, that was never very long. Until the punitive expeditions disbanded, the Indians lived on cactus seed and clams, then returned to their raiding on shore. But if any Yori, or white man, ventured into their desert hunting ground, sooner or later they hung his scalp on a pole.

They are a tall and slender people, a nation of runners; and so proud were they of their warlike courage that they often left their weapons behind, killing their enemies with their bare hands. They ran down the horses of the settlers on the desert, springing on their withers like mountain lions and breaking their necks with one twist. The flesh they ate raw, and drank the blood—as proper a race of savages as the world has ever seen.

The approach to this desert land is through a forest of thorny trees, interspersed with four species of giant

cacti and many spiny shrubs. Yet through this waste-
land the Seris run barefoot, seldom seen unless they
wish to be seen. This great plain is really the delta of
two mountain streams, down which every year or so
there comes a wide-spreading flood, rushing on till it
reaches the Gulf.

To catch this water, the cactus spreads its roots far
out; while the mesquite trees and ironwoods send a
long tap-root straight down, to reach the underflow.
Between floods, the plain is bone dry, crisscrossed in
every direction by washes and channels along which
the road winds and twists. From Nogales and the
border to Hermosillo is a hundred and fifty miles; and
it is sixty miles further to Kino Bay, where the last of
the Seris now live.

As long as they stayed on the Island, close contact
with the tribe was impossible; but in 1930 a club of
Arizona sportsmen brought them out of their strong-
hold in a day. While the Indians looked on from the
beach of Tiburon, a huge bird came flying down from
the north and landed at Kino Bay. It was an airplane
from Tucson, the first they had ever seen, and two
strange men stepped off. These Americans were scout-
ing the country for fishing and hunting and, when
they built a Lodge on the shore, the whole Seri nation
moved over.

The last white man to build a house there had been
murdered in cold blood—Fray Cristomo Gil, in 1772.
But he had been a missionary, trying to teach them
the catechism. These fishermen and hunters were gen-
erous with what they caught, giving the Indians a
good half of everything, with a drink out of the black
bottle to boot. That settled it with the Seris—the most

arrant beggars in the world—and they camped down by the Lodge to stay.

They were still there when we visited them in January, 1932; but hard times had come, the Hunting Lodge had closed down and they found themselves on the beach. Instead of sponging on the hunters, they had to work for what they got, for a Greek fish merchant had taken over the concession and he made them get out and fish. Mr. Corona was friendly to the Indians, but he thought it was better for them to work than to beg—especially as they had very few guests at the Lodge to beg from.

The Seris are good fishermen and were doing very well until, about a month before we came, the sea bass suddenly stopped biting and the Indians had to gather oysters for a living. These were found in the Lagoon, three miles down the beach, and the pay was one peso for a five-gallon can of solid meats. Very little, of course, but it would keep them alive until the fish began to bite. When we drove in with two heavily loaded cars we found the whole tribe assembled at the sheds, cracking oysters with irons, scooping out the luscious meats and staring with not unfriendly eyes.

After our rough trip from the Border our hearts leapt with joy as we beheld these primitive creatures. The men were dark and grim, with a predatory look; the women more gentle, though ragged beyond belief. At first sight they seemed quite Oriental in appearance, and their cheeks were beautifully decorated with face-paintings. They were still, apparently, almost as wild as when they had left Tiburon; and we hoped to find, treasured away behind those low brows, the lore of an ancient people—if we could only get them to talk!

No beggars in a play could be half as motley—they seemed to have made a study of patches and rags. But, no matter how scantily they were dressed, every man wore a loincloth like an apron—usually a red bandanna handkerchief. This was a holdover from their Island days, when their sole attire had been the skin of a pelican. Cast-off shirts and pants had been adopted later, but they did not consider themselves dressed without these cloths about their hips. It gave the effect of a Malay sarong—a last, barbaric touch.

The women wore long skirts of cheap cotton, with a short blouse barely covering the breast, and a handkerchief over the hair. Otherwise their only ornamentation was the blue-and-white clan-paintings across their cheeks. They sat in the middle of their family groups, their voices soft and low—like the *quah, quah,* of contented hens—as they admired Lady's red hat. It was at once their envy and despair, since they were too poor to buy one like it and didn't wear hats, anyway!

They named her Red Hat on the spot, the other member of the family being called Big Beard. But for our guide, John Hampton, on whom we had counted so much, there was not a single look of recognition. Twenty years before he had lived among them under the name of El Americano. The symbol of the Turtle Clan had been painted on his cheeks and he had known the old war chief, Juan Tomas'. But Juan was not there, nobody knew him, and he was badly hacked.

Hampton was a botanist and a scientist, whose work had taken him to the ends of the world since we had met at Hermosillo during the Revolution. He spoke Spanish fluently and accurately and it was through his advice that we had ventured on this trip. Now he stood in the presence of fifty or sixty Seris, a good half of the tribe, and not one would admit that he knew him. For the first time he realized how long twenty years is, when a man leaves and never comes back.

Mr. Corona, the fish merchant, was in full charge at Kino Bay, the former manager having just left, and he made us welcome at the Lodge. He had a good cook, too, but all we would eat that first day was oysters. They were absolutely fresh, having been brought up that morning in canoes, and the most delicious we had ever tasted. Corona was sealing them in cans and sending them by truck to the railroad, just to keep the Indians busy until the sea bass began to bite again.

After lunch we returned to the sheds, to stare and be stared at, and never had we seen Indians more intelligent-looking, or more given to lighthearted laughter. The women, all jabbering at once, were positively gay. That was a good sign, for it showed they were friendly. From the reports of McGee and Kroeber, the principal anthropologists who had visited them, we had gathered that the Seris were very fierce—the lowest savages in North America, still living in the Stone Age. But, after watching them a while, we decided there had been some mistake.

We could see that they were lousy by the way they scratched, but all savages are that. What we noticed most was the kind and gentle way in which the mothers handled their children, who were never punished for anything. The men seemed to have little to say, which went to prove what Hampton had told us, that they were living under a form of matriarchy. They worked away stolidly, cracking the oysters for the women to shuck, looking us over with unblinking eyes, but making no attempt to beg.

Not one of our interpreter's old friends was there,

to give us the welcome he had promised, so we drove up the beach to the Indians' camp. It was nothing but a collection of huts, built of brush piled on frames of ocotillo cactus; and, from a distance could hardly be distinguished from the sand dunes. But when we walked out to the camp we could see their boats along the shore, and a hundred mongrel dogs rushed forth.

It was hard to believe that a people who had so little to eat could support so many worthless curs. There was no food of any kind in sight, and the brush shelters were practically empty. No beds, no boxes, no clothes—only a hole in the middle for a tiny fire at night and, between that and the wall, just room enough for the family to sleep. They cooked out-of-doors, wore their clothes day and night; and used their blankets, when they had any, as mantles.

Old sea-turtle shells were laid against the outer walls to break the force of the chilly north wind, and hardly a person was in sight. Only a blind man, sitting alone; a woman with a basket of wood on her head returning from the inland forest; a distant fisherman, caulking his boat. But here at last Hampton found a Seri who knew him—Angelita Encinas, his clan mother. Twenty years before, when they had been working for him, she had painted the turtle symbol on his cheeks and taught him certain words to speak. He had forgotten all the words, but when he gave her a string of beads her face lighted up with a smile of recognition.

She was a kindly looking woman and spoke a little Spanish; and as they sat down together, inquiring after each other's families, she seemed like an old New England aunt. While they were talking, her husband returned—Manuel, very deaf. He was one of three men that Hampton had been looking for, but the old chief could not remember him. Until, after a lot of shouting, John presented him with a pack of cigarettes, which helped his memory wonderfully. He rose up and gave him the Mexican hug, or *abrazo,* and we concluded that all was well.

It was ten days since we had left the Border, with the idea of making friends with these Indians and seeing what true savages are like, and for the last three we had been camped at a neighboring ranch, waiting for John's friends to come. We wanted to get them away from the rest, where we could question them undisturbed; but, though he sent repeated messages, not a Seri had appeared. Now at last he had found Manuel, and they talked together for an hour; but when Hampton returned to the car he reported that Encinas would not come.

"Very sorry," he said. "They are going to have a Fish Dance to make the sea bass bite, and he has to take the part of the Grandfather. It begins tonight and lasts for four days. We will have to go back to the ranch and wait."

"But why can't we move over here," pleaded Red Hat, "and observe them in their native habitat? And then we could see the Fish Dance!"

"You don't realize," he said, "how wild these Indians are—and what a dangerous bunch of camp-robbers! But of course, if you insist—"

We had engaged Americano to be our guide and interpreter, and were supposed to defer to his judgment; but ten days of mishaps and camping at deserted ranches had rather dashed our confidence. It was very impolite, but we insisted. We just had to see the Fish Dance!

CHAPTER II

The Fish Dance

NOT in a year had the Seris given their dance to placate the great Fish God, the whale, and every fish in the sea. But the sea bass had stopped biting in the middle of their season and, the day before we had arrived, Santo Blanco, the medicine man, had announced:

"Tomorrow night again we will dance."

"*Ahn-kwee'p-ay*—it is good!" the people answered; and Manuel had to take the part of Old Man, in the Round Dance given by the girls. We took it as a good sign that we should arrive among them on the very day of the dance. All the outside Seris would be in, and we would be received as guests. It would be a gala day, and the tribal hospitality would protect us from any harm. So we put up at the cold and scantily furnished Lodge and, as the evening came on, we went out to see the sunset.

Kino Bay, when the sun sets across the Gulf, is spectacular in its beauty. In a succession of golden loomings, the mirage reveals islands never seen by day, they are so far beyond the curve of the world. Except during a storm the water is smooth and calm, and the Seris have compared the reflections on its surface to the paintings on a woman's face.

As the sun went down the full moon came up behind us, a yellow disk in the east; but the Indian village was dark. There is something about white sand at night that seems to take up the light, and the Seris were sparing with their wood. The women had brought it on their heads for miles, and their fires had to last all night.

If we had had any doubts about our welcome they were dispelled as we stumbled into camp. Their young chief, Chico Romero, showed us a place to sit, and the women invited Red Hat into their houses. They seemed really pleased to have us attend the festival; but we sat very still—not to disturb the ceremonies—while from the semidarkness there came the voice of Santo Blanco, the medicine man who could talk with God.

He sat with his back against the chief's house and his face to the sea, a dim form in the black shadow, speaking for all the people. He is a sturdy little man, with mild, dreamy eyes, more or less afraid of the turbulent war chiefs, but secure in the protection of the gods. To his right, and facing him, a burly young Seri stood on a plank, keeping time for the singer with the rub-a-dub-dub of bare feet, while he leaned his weight on a staff.

In the early days they had used half the shell of a sea turtle, set over a hollow in the sand; but the plank sounded like a drum and could be heard a mile away. Santo Blanco began to shake his rattles—made of milk cans thrust through with wooden handles and containing grains of corn—and they gave out a silvery chime, like the ching-ching-ching of sleigh bells. Then Martín Villalobo, the dancer, thumped off a rhythmic beat; and, in a low voice, the singer began.

His songs were addressed to every fish in the sea in turn, and if any was forgotten the whole dance would come to nothing. For four nights, from dark to dawn, the little man must sit and sing. Each song had a different tune, a different rhythm for the dancer, different words to appease the fish deities.

Meanwhile in the outer darkness, ignored by everybody, Juan Molino sang a song to the deer. The same song all night, lest Venado be offended if they sang to the fishes and not to him. Leaning forward, with rattles in both hands, he danced on a worn-out calfskin, while his accompanist rasped a rod across the notches of a larger stick. The lower end rested upon the bottom of an inverted basket and it made a noise like the croaking of frogs.

THE SONG OF THE DEER

The deer is hungry.
He goes through the bushes
Till he finds an ironwood in flower.
He eats the green leaves
And the flowers and says:
"Now I am not hungry.
I have eaten of the green
And I have eaten of the flowers."

I will go out to hunt.
I will go out to kill a deer.
I will kill him quickly.
The sound of my voice
Does not reach the deer.
I will sing louder and he will come.
He comes closer! Now he is near
And I kill him quickly.

Later in the evening, and nearer the water, a Round Dance was performed, presided over by Manuel Encinas, as the Grandfather. In a circle not five feet

Santo Blanco singing the Fish Chant while a young Seri stands on a plank, keeping time with the rub-a-dub-dub of bare feet.

(Photograph by Dane Coolidge)

Juan Tomas, the old war chief, gazed at us doubtfully with his maimed left hand to his lips. But when Americano produced a package of cigarettes, the old renegade fell on his neck.

(Photograph by James W. Manson)

across, all the young, unmarried girls danced around him, leaning forward as they held out their skirts from their knees and sang a childish chorus. It sounded like a group of schoolgirls, singing their morning song, with the old man's deep voice below.

They sang to the whale, the Chief of all the Fishes, and to sea animals and sea birds—but not to land birds and animals—and made merry as they danced. It was like dancing around the Maypole with us, and with all the little girls in front and the older girls in circles behind. All the songs had a short, well-defined melody, with a very catchy way of swinging back to the first line and ending with it for a chorus. It was very sophisticated music to be sung by savages, far more like ours than like that of the pastoral Navajos; and the intricate rhythms of the plank-dancers would put our tap-dancers to shame. Yet they executed their steps flat-footed, without resorting to heel-and-toe.

One of the most beautiful of Santo Blanco's Fish Dance songs was:

SONG OF THE SEA

The wind blows over me.
It blows from all sides.
It blows from everywhere.

The wind blows over me.
It blows strong.
My waves pile the seaweed
On the shore.

The wind blows over me.
I roll great waves on the shore.

I roll more waves and more waves
And more waves from the wind.

When the wind blows over me
My waves throw the shellfish
And shells on the shore.
Like a sand dune the shells pile up.

When the wind does not blow
I make no waves
And the sea is calm and smooth.
In the night the wind does not blow.

Only soft breezes blow.
The sea is calm.
In the day the wind comes strong
The sea is rough.

In the early morning
A light breeze blows.
All the sea is calm.

At midday the turtle
Swims on the surface.
He sleeps with his head out.
At midday the wind blows strong,
The turtle goes below.

For eight days the wind does not blow.
The sea is calm.
The whales and porpoise,
Turtles and fish,
Are happy.
Their heads look out from the sea.

Quite in the modern way, the song paints the changing moods of the sea, speaking first in the person of the sea and then of the singer himself. Chico Romero told us that these songs are very old, dating back to the Old Seris who first occupied the Island, three thousand years ago. We could tell from the soft, rapt tones of the singer that they had a poetic import; and as we listened we strained our eyes through the darkness to make out the lines of his face.

Something told us that here was the very man we sought, for with Indians the medicine men are the intellectuals of the tribe—the priests, the poets, the historians. No matter how rough and brutal the rest may be, these men who "talk with God" have developed their spiritual nature through years of fasting and prayer. But that spirituality must be recognized and respected or they will never break their reserve. Santo Blanco was a good man, we knew by his gentle, vibrant voice, and we resolved to make him our friend.

It was bitterly cold on that wind-swept shore, and as the night wore on the women and children retired to their brush houses; but we stayed, reluctant to go. Then, out of the darkness, Manuel appeared leading Juan Tomas', the war chief, the second of Hampton's three friends. As Manuel came closer, he pointed to Americano, who rose up and held out his hand; but Juan Tomas' gazed at him doubtfully. He was an old man and hard to win over; a famous warrior, who had killed many men; but when Hampton drew out a package of cigarettes the old renegade fell on his neck.

"*Amigo*—my friend!" he cried; and clasped him to his breast. It was going pretty far for Hampton to take this old scoundrel in his arms, but he hugged him affectionately and kissed him on both cheeks, while all the Seris smiled.

"Da me cigarros!" shouted the war chief as he finally broke his hold; and John gave him another pack. The old Seris smoked a short clay pipe, like an Irish dudeen; but they have learned to like the Mexican *cigarros* and "give me some cigarettes" is the standard approach of all beggars. Of these Juan Tomas' proved himself the most extortionate. It is through just such insistent demands as this that their quarrels with white people begin—but Hampton got through it without a bobble by giving him his third and last pack. Juan felt over him carefully, gave his pockets another pat, and, convinced that there were no more, the situation was saved.

We returned to the Lodge shortly afterwards, leaving the dancers to sing out the night.

CHAPTER III

The Three Old Friends

WE HAD had our way about staying to the Fish Dance; but the next day, when we wanted to camp near the village, John Hampton would not permit it. He knew the Seris, and their reputation as camp-robbers, and we camped half a mile away—down the beach behind a sand dune, on the east side of the Lodge. Even then, but for the vigilance of Angelito, our Mexican cook and camp-tender who had followed us on horseback, we would have been overwhelmed.

They came in droves as we began to make camp, but he had hacked out the heart of a huge mangrove tree—where the sand, drifting in, had built up a wall against the branch tips—and had stored everything out of their reach. Then he called Es-sport, his dog; picked up his 30-30 rifle; and laid a stick across the brushy entrance. That was a sign the Indians knew —and Angelito knew *them*. He had been a soldier in the Revolution, and had been on one expedition to the Island, so they decided to stay out of his kitchen.

Hampton parked his car at the foot of the sand dune and set up his auto tent, while we pitched ours in the lee of a neighboring mangrove and hurried out to see the second night of the Fish Dance. It was cold, with a bitter north wind, but Santo Blanco was in his place against the chief's house, still singing his songs of the sea. Most of the women and children had retired early, after the ceremonies had begun, and we

31

were glad to get back to camp. Only an Indian could endure singing four nights in succession; but Santo Blanco, though he had been working all day, sang on till dawn.

After a long cold night we were up at daylight, and we were just finishing our breakfast by Angelito's fire when a man and woman appeared at the entrance. It was Santo Blanco and his wife, carrying her baby; and as they stood looking in at our cozy kitchen, he could hardly keep his eyes open. All that night he had been singing to bring back the sea bass; and now he and his wife were on their way to the lagoon to dig up oysters to crack.

It was against all the rules for handling savages as laid down by our mentor and guide, but they looked so cold and wistful that we rose up and beckoned them in. Hampton was still asleep, Angelito could not dismiss them; so we had our own way once more and fed them all they could eat. Plates full of hot rice, covered with condensed milk and sugar—more coffee, more jerked beef. It is almost a religion with the Seris never to store any food. They eat all they have and then go hungry until they can gather more.

But just as our guests were leaving another Indian appeared, and Angelito reached for his gun. It was Buro Alazan, Americano's third friend, though we did not know that then. He was a predatory-looking old party and loomed big at the entrance, but we smiled and beckoned him in. If you are going to be friends with Indians you have got to feed them when they are hungry; but we learned afterward that the old war chief had an evil reputation, having killed two Americans on Tiburon.

But this was the mainland, and Roan Mule-deer

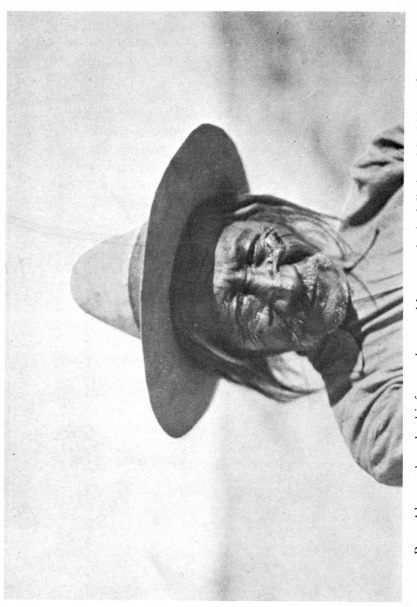

Buro Alazan, the sub-chief, a predatory old party who had distinguished himself during the killing of two Americans on Tiburon.

(Photograph by Dane Coolidge)

Little girls walk solemnly along with the procession, learning to carry small burdens on their head-rings. (Photograph by Dane Coolidge)

The Seri women carry their wood on their heads, beginning young. (Photograph by Dane Coolidge)

was too hungry to take advantage of our ignorance. All he wanted was something to eat, and we had cooked up lots of it. He was just stalking out of camp when Hampton, who was a late sleeper, emerged from his auto tent; and, at sight of his old friend, Buro Alazan made a rush and gathered him into his arms.

"Ah, *amigo!*" he cried. *"Lo mismo!* We are the same!"

There was no escape for poor Americano, though we could see he was getting about enough of it. He returned the embrace of this burly giant, who was repeating that they were equals—that is, brothers. But, after the first ecstasy of his joy had passed, Buro felt Hampton over with expert hands and shouted roughly:

"Da me cigarros!"

John gave him the cigarettes which he had already located, and Angelito took advantage of the Boss's presence to replace the barrier to his kitchen. So all was in order when Americano entered and called for his belated breakfast.

Santo Blanco hurried away down the trail to the lagoon, for he had eight daughters to provide for and they would be waiting when he got home. They lived from hand to mouth, from meal to meal, and in hard times they did not eat at all. But with it all they managed to look healthy and happy. Perhaps all the weak ones had died off.

With the appearance of Hampton the rush for a free breakfast ceased, though women and children came and sat about. Until their men-folks poled up from the lagoon with the canoe-loads of oysters there was nothing for them to do and, while Red Hat made her toilette in the sleeping tent, quite an audience gathered outside. The Seri women are like curious children, wanting to see everything the Yoris had and did, and hoping she would give them something.

When she heard faint whisperings in front of her tent, Red Hat untied the flaps and found herself facing half a dozen brown women and babies, sitting in the sand and waiting for the show. She combed out her hair and went on with the details of dressing. Then, as they saw her good, warm clothes, they held out their poor rags and said;

"*Manta!*"

They were begging for cloth, to mend their worn garments, for they were miserably cold; but this was a demand we had not anticipated and she could only tell them No. Hampton made them understand that she had only one change of clothing and none to spare, however much they needed it; so they just sighed and felt of her warm coat wishfully.

In the cold, almost freezing wind, most of them wore only a two-piece garment—a full, long skirt and a loose blouse without a belt, made of the flimsiest cotton flannel, originally of some bright color but now faded and dirty and ragged. A tall, graceful young married woman was conspicuous in a new dress of brilliant cerise cotton flannel with the folds wrapped around her legs for warmth. This was the type of dress they had adopted from the Yaquis, at the time when McGee pictured them—in place of their traditional costume, the picturesque skirt of pelican skins.

With a credit ticket at the Commissary of one peso for a five-gallon tin full of shelled oysters, few women could buy enough for a whole dress at one time. Most of them would buy a yard or two and tog it onto the tattered remnants of the ones they were wearing, mak-

ing themselves a crazy-quilt garment. Such under-
garments as they had were made of cotton floursacks.
They needed clothing so much that, when fishing
barques and Coast steamers occasionally anchored off
the Island, they paddled out and begged for it, and
complained because the tourists gave them money instead.

When the women understood that Red Hat had no
manta to give they showed the holes in their ragged
dresses and begged for needles and thread. She gave
all she had and, when the supply was exhausted, sent
to Hermosillo by the fish-truck driver for more.
Among his many commissions—mail, money, provisions—he brought back a lot of darning needles and
spools of coarse cotton thread.

To a folded scrap of paper she tied the end of the
thread while, just as her grandmother had done for
her, she held the spool and motioned each woman to
wind off as much as she wanted. They laughed and
were apparently satisfied.

After that the women began to bring in domestic
implements to sell; polishing stones, hairbrushes made
of fiber, cutting stones, awls for basket weaving, and
pretty shells picked up on the beach. We bought them,
every one, at whatever price. Usually twenty centavos
or a hunk of *panoche* sugar was enough. We had explained that we wanted "old things"; but we took
whatever they offered, since we needed their good
will.

We wished to learn everything these women could
tell us; and all the more because investigators rarely
get any information directly from primitive women.
They are shy and relatively inarticulate—the men do
all the chanting and storytelling and it is improper for

young Indian women to be seen talking with white men.

Although they were beggars, we found the Seri women very gentle and trustworthy, with none of the violent ways that made the warriors so dangerous; but hardly had Red Hat made friends with them than Juan Tomas' appeared on the scene. Hampton laid out a piece of canvas for him to sit on and came through with the rest of his *cigarros;* and when Buro Alazan, the sub-chief, arrived he gave him another seat of honor.

It was very important to placate these war chiefs, for they were capable of doing great mischief; and Americano passed the cigarettes around to all the other warriors. But just as his reception was going nicely, Juan Tomas' rose up, tucked the camp canvas under his shirt and broke into a run up the trail. And, while Hampton was looking after him, Buro Alazan started off the other way, likewise with his canvas under his shirt. But John was so enraged by this breach of friendship that he chased after him and snatched it back.

"I thought you gave it to me!" protested Buro, to save his face; but the other Indians all laughed.

"I gave it to you to sit on!" came back Hampton; but now he too had lost face. The two old friends whom he had embraced and presented with cigarettes, had turned out to be common thieves and camp-robbers, who would steal anything in sight. It was a terrible humiliation, after all he had promised us, but Manuel Encinas saved the day.

CHAPTER IV

Seri Customs and Manners

MANUEL was a true friend, and above such petty thievery; and when he and Angelita came down for their visit, a bargain was quickly struck. As the sociologist of the party, Red Hat made haste to engage him to tell about their customs and manners; and, though he was getting senile, he made it plain at the start that he considered himself far superior to the war chiefs.

"Juan Tomas' and good old Buro Alazan," he said, "are good men, but they are no longer strong. I am old, the same as they are, but I can still bring water. I can still kill the buro-deer and the sea lion, but they are getting soft."

Encinas was an honest old fellow and, with the advice and assistance of his wife, who was clan mother of the Turtle Clan, he described the marriage customs of his people.

The family of the boy goes to the mother of the girl and, in the presence of her relatives, proposes that they talk it over. If the mother agrees, the girl's father presents the proposal to the girl herself; and during several days there is discussion of the economic circumstances of the boy. But, if the girl objects, all negotiations cease—"She only marries of her own free will."

If the suitor is approved he brings evidences—not gifts—of his circumstances, of his ability to support a wife, and is accepted on probation. He is then at the beck and call of his future mother-in-law. He lives with her household as a provider, but he has no status as a married man and sleeps outside the shelter. The mother-in-law makes him do "much work" and he is virtually a servant. On other occasions, whenever this was mentioned, everybody laughed. Manuel Encinas said the period of probation—engagement—was a year; other narrators said many months. But as the Seris have no definite calendar and only vaguely understand Spanish reckoning, it must be assumed that the length of the period is indefinite or is likely to be ended with the cactus-pear season, when most marriages take place.

When the boy has acquired the necessary property —much money, a canoe, dried meat and fish, pelican skins or clothes or other useful goods—he goes, accompanied by his mother, to the bride's house. The mother-in-law sits on the left of the entrance, the girl in the center and the boy takes his seat on the right. This is the public ceremony of marriage. The young couple may decide to build a separate shelter attached to the family house, but they often live with the girl's family.

There was an ancient custom, so Encinas said, that when the bridegroom came to the new house for the completion of the marriage, he was beaten by the women, "but this is no longer done."

Marriage is generally monogamous—all the story-tellers at one interview or another agreed—but Encinas added, "if the wife is willing and the husband can support another, he may take two." Santo Blanco gave us examples. Porfirio Diaz, the old coyote-faced man who lived in the last shelter, used to have two wives. Now he has none, only many daughters. There was a man up the Coast who had two wives.

The women all object if a man wants to take another woman; they never let him have two together in one house. Nacho Romero tried to have two wives, but the women took one of them away from him. Nacho was just a fisherman and not rich and the girl now has a baby and is living alone, next to her mother. This girl is Ramona and she is very good-looking. She is the only girl who has ever been away to school and learned to read and write.

We were surprised to discover that there are girls and women who do not wish to get married. Santo Blanco has three daughters and Chief Chico one, who will not marry. Candelaria, one of the old women we saw, is mentioned by McGee in 1894 as "the belle of the Seri." At the command of her mother, Juana Maria, she allowed her picture to be painted; but now she is getting old and drinks a good deal. "Many have wanted her, but she would not marry."

Santo Blanco said: "No matter how drunk, none of these women have intercourse with men. The Greek who works in the store tries to get the Seri women, but they will have nothing to do with him." Later evidence showed, however, that at least two of them were prostitutes.

Either husband or wife may divorce the partner and go back to his or her own family, but divorce was said to be uncommon. Whether the pair have children or not seems to have no relation to divorce, or the taking of a second wife.

A puberty feast is held for girls. At the first sign of womanhood the tribe prepares for a dance, bringing fruit and vegetable food, but not meat or fish. The

girl must not eat meat or fish for eight days. All—
men, women and young people—dance for four days
at the first full moon after her puberty. Then she is
regarded as a marriageable woman.

Encinas could not recite the dance songs, of which
he said there were a great number. The Seris have a
ceremonial in May "in hot weather when the pelicans
on Tiburon sleep," the greatest of the year, when
marriages usually occur. They make wine of *pitahaya*
cactus fruit and "the women get a little drunk."

There were some indications that maturity came
late. There was a girl who had been born at Santa Ana
Rancho when El Americano and his wife were living
there in the summer of 1913, who was now, in 1932,
just reaching maturity. It was impossible to find out
why girls refuse to marry—it may be that some of
them had not reached maturity. Buro Alazan explained
that "as long as a young man has a father living, he
must not marry."

Quite unexpectedly Manuel Encinas, in answer to
some question about sickness, told us the following
dramatic story of his experience in an influenza epi-
demic.

When influenza came it came to Pedro and his
tall sons, the three tallest men in the tribe. It came
from the east. Nobody saw it come, but Pedro lay
many days, getting weaker and weaker with cough
and fever. The sickness visited many of the Seris, until
Manuel Encinas himself became ill. All these sick
people stayed inside their houses.

One night when Encinas had been sick ten-plus-
ten days he was lying in his house and could not sleep.
He looked out into the night where the moon was
shining, and saw a very skinny old man, walking with

a crooked stick, coming from a distance. The old man hobbled along, peering from side to side, and when he found sick people in their houses he pointed his stick at their breasts, and they died.

When Manuel Encinas saw this figure he immediately crawled out of his house, holding up his hands and supplicating the moon; and the crouching, skinny figure put his forearm over his eyes and hobbled away and didn't touch Manuel with his stick. And so he didn't die.

Old Encinas turned to the interpreter and added:

"I am old and you are old; but those who didn't come out of their houses, died!"

All that day and the next, Red Hat and El Americano sat out in the brilliant sunshine, extracting from Manuel and Angelita what they could about Seri family customs. But unfortunately they had become the center of interest for all the idle Indians in camp. They listened in on everything, often correcting the speakers; until at last a large office tent was put up and furnished with an old table from the Lodge.

When the storyteller of the day took his place, sitting on a box by the table, Big Beard was called in to do the writing while Red Hat stood guard at the door. Admitting first the men leaders and the matrons, she kept the crowd outside by tying up the flaps. But conditions were far from ideal. The five leading men were very jealous of each other; and the old women murmured running comments.

It was a tedious and exhausting performance for all —for the storyteller, who spoke in crude Spanish; for the interpreter who had to question him before he was sure of the meaning; and no less for Big Beard who, before writing it down, asked more questions in Span-

ish and English. But when the working routine had
been established, the visitors began to understand they
must not disturb the speakers, and we went ahead
with better results.

When the men were at last occupied and the idlers
turned away, Red Hat was free to go to the fish-sheds,
where the Seri women were shucking oysters, to be
shipped two or three times a week to Hermosillo and
the Arizona markets. The women sat on the sand,
suckling their children and trying to get warm at the
oil-drum stove, after several hours of standing in the
icy waters of the oyster lagoon. For filling a five-gallon can full of solid meats, they were paid one peso—
at that time thirty-five cents in silver—by Pedro, the
Greek in charge, and then went to the little Commissary at the Lodge to spend it for flour, beans and
sugar. The few pesos each could earn did not buy
much provisions for a family of five to eight people,
and nothing at all of the *manta* and other domestic
comforts they wanted.

Toward midday they went back to the brush village
on the brow of the sandy shore, to do their housekeep-
ing. Day after day Red Hat wandered along after
them or sat down to watch them work. By this time
they were used to seeing her at the tents and, though
shy as always, they were friendly enough and behaved
as if they scarcely saw her. The little brush huts, built
of ocotillo ribs and supported at the sides with big
turtle shells or rocks, clung together in groups like
wasps' nests, on the brow of the beach. In front of
them were small fires of ironwood, which burns with
little flame and is very hot, where housewives broiled
fresh fish on the coals or cooked beans in an earthen
pot.

In the old days on Tiburon they often ate their meat raw, having no matches with which to start fires. Seeds ground up by means of rocks then provided an edible gruel or mush, but now more and more they were making pan-bread of white flour, or boiling flour with *panoche* sugar—when they could get it. Their rocky island and the ancient hunting ground on the mainland, afforded two luxuries—cactus-pears in summer, and venison. There were then many deer, which they killed with bow and arrows or by running them down. When we saw them they were unusually poverty-stricken—until the sea bass began to bite.

One day Red Hat saw a horse staked out by the village, which we were told had been bought at Escalante Rancho. It broke loose and a young Seri vaquero, who was evidently quite unable to handle it, ran it down and finally killed it. A day or two later its hide was drying on the top of a house; and its skull, picked clean, lay near by. The American rancher at Costa Rica had spoken warmly of a Seri woman who worked for him at a dollar a day to pay for two mares and a stallion, which she took down to the Gulf. At low tide the Indians got the animals across the Straits to the Island and there turned them loose to increase. The Seris have no domestic animals except dogs, but covet horses and cattle and have been known to steal them from the ranchers. But if unmolested they might soon become pastoral, as the Navajos did when they acquired stock from the natives of New Mexico.

Their bodies are very dirty, but not as filthy and odorous as might be expected when it is remembered that they never have had easy access to fresh water. On Tiburon Island, their age-long home, there is only one considerable spring for the whole tribe, and on

the mainland no fresh water within five to eight miles
of the shore. They have always camped far from
water, which is found only in the mountains, while
their home is along the beach. At Kino Bay they have
to go five miles inland through a thorny forest and
carry water home on their heads in an oil-tin which,
when full, weighs forty pounds.

We brought water for ourselves in cans on the running-board of an automobile, or bought a little from
the fish dealer. The Fish Company brought water for
their own use in large, emptied gasoline drums, and
the manager was angry because the Indians stole
water from them. Sometimes Indian women cut grama
grass for his saddle horses, to pay for a little water.
But we seldom saw them washing their children or
their clothes, or even their hands and food, except in
salt water. They cleaned their few pots and pans with
dry sand; and, when they had fresh water, washed the
babies' clothes first. Yet somehow their faces were
fairly clean.

On any morning Red Hat would see half a dozen
women disappearing into the forest with their empty
oil-tins. By old deer and cattle trails they went through
the mesquite brush, to get wood and water for the day.
Everything is carried by women on a head-ring made
of split swamp-willow, wrapped with fiber or old rags.
On this ring the tin full of water is mounted, and the
more skillful carriers do not even steady it with the
hand as they walk the miles homeward.

Since the Yoris have begun to come in for hunting
and fishing, the forest is receding and the women have
to go farther for their wood supply. They break it off
in three- or four-foot lengths and pile it in a large,
coarse basket-tray which is set on top of the head-ring.

One woman helps another to poise her load but, once started, she walks several miles without putting it down. Toward noon the procession of wood and water gatherers emerges from the forest, walking steadily down the long sandy slope. Young and old, they are all graceful, sure of movement, straight and incredibly strong. Occasionally little girls walk solemnly along with the procession, learning to carry small burdens on their head-rings.

Those who stayed at home were cooking, cleaning fish and spreading them on the houses to dry, or mending the wind-torn shelters; suckling children or weaving baskets; but chiefly dressing hair—their own, or the children's or their husbands'. Combing, brushing with a fiber brush, braiding and tying it with fiber string made of mesquite-roots. One day Buro Alazan and his tall old wife sat on the sand in front of their house, she brushing and braiding his hair—he is a very vain old fellow—and he in turn brushing and braiding hers. But they do not wash it in soapweed suds, nor keep it as sleek and shining as the Pueblos and Navajos do.

They must be very lousy, for the children are always scratching; and, since the families sleep together with their feet toward the center, vermin and infection would be inevitable. But Chief Romero says they have no venereal diseases, perhaps because the women do not consort with white men. Their skin is a beautiful dark yellow-brown, smooth and without blemish. Their hands are small, and their feet large, splayed out with much walking in desert sand. The tribe is steadily diminishing—in former years because of many wars and lately from influenza and measles.

The living children appear to be from two to two

and a half years apart. Encinas told us that when a woman has a child she does not have another for a long time, and Santo Blanco said the men were instructed not to approach their wives too soon after childbirth. But it seems probable that, as among most Indian tribes, a large number of children die in infancy.

Some weeks after we arrived a bootlegger, ostensibly a fisherman, camped near the Lodge and sold mezcal to the Indians. Many were drunk and two days later an old man died, after a brawl. He was buried secretly that night, and four houses at that end of camp were at once abandoned, the families moving over to a new spot. White flags of mourning were set up around the village and that afternoon a few women were wailing—making a sound almost like yodeling, while the neighbors ate their supper indifferently.

It is the prerogative of matrons to locate the shelters, under the direction of the Elderwoman then in power. There was apparently some dispute over the relocation. Chico Romero, sitting in front of his house, was being harangued by two old women. Encinas' wife talked shrilly, waving her arms. Santo Blanco's wife stood up and talked rapidly at every interval. Occasionally two or three other matrons took their turns. The Chief listened for half an hour, scarcely spoke, and finally walked away. The next day the new houses were built, but which party won the argument we did not learn.

All day long children from five to twelve years old played on the sand dunes, with a horde of mongrel dogs, laughing often but almost never crying or screaming. Indeed, the Seris laugh more than any Indians we have ever known. Babies look messy and

The Little Seri children play on the sand dunes all day, almost never crying. There is no visible discipline, they do not have to go to school or have their faces washed.

(Photograph by Dane Coolidge)

After the Fish Dance the sea bass began to run abundantly.

(Photograph by Dane Coolidge)

miserable but seldom cry, and are nursed until they are two or three years old. If the mother has not enough milk, some other woman suckles them. These children of all ages were quite modest about their habits, retiring into the brush on occasion and seldom exposing their persons. There was no visible discipline. If a child got hurt it was comforted; if it showed temper it was generally ignored, or shaken a little and then left to have its cry out. Since they got nothing by screaming, not even attention, they seldom screamed.

No girls, not even women, except the old, went anywhere alone. They were with the family, or under the village eye, all the time and thus sufficiently protected. As far as we could learn, only two young women of the tribe had a questionable reputation. Ramona, the mistress of Nacho Romero, was now living alone, because the matrons were violently opposed to any man taking a second wife. The other was a young woman who went out in a fishing boat overnight and whom we saw brought into camp screaming drunk. She was met on the shore by an old man and her mother, who dragged her into the house. The matrons were apparently scandalized.

With strange men coming to the Lodge and to the Fish Company headquarters, and with liquor sold openly—although against the Mexican law—it is surprising that prostitution is not more common. In the afternoons a few men, women and boys were gambling in the village, using green sticks, matches and beans for counters and a piece of braid to mark the dealer.

Toward sunset every evening we walked along the half-moon beach, to enjoy the glory of the skies that faced us beyond Isla Tassne and Tiburon. When the fishing boats began to come in, women and children ran down to help pull up the clumsy, leaking crafts and to claim the family's share of the catch. After the Fish Dance the fish began to run abundantly, and the people were no longer hungry. While the boatmen stowed the gear and threw out the fish, women cut off the heads and fins, which the hungry dogs made off with. These sea bass weighed about forty pounds apiece, and two were as much as a man could carry on the ends of a pole over his shoulder. The women cooked some immediately, for the men had been out since daylight. As night fell, the fires died down; little piles of coals twinkled and glimmered in front of the brush shelters, and shortly they all went to bed, curled up together and wrapped in all their clothing.

Always we lingered to take in the long twilight scene—one of the most beautiful, it must be, any-where on the West Coast. Often just before sunset a fairy mirage of unseen islands across the Gulf of California rose on the far horizon and faded away into the sea. In the clear, dry air the outlines of Tiburon, and the perfect curve of the desert beach, came out sharply; while the dim mountain ranges of Lower California far beyond, disappeared. The enigma of primitive human life was blotted out in the serenity of the glamorous Southern night.

CHAPTER V

The War Chief Talks

ALL was well, with Manuel telling stories and
Americano interpreting them into English,
when suddenly our storyteller quit. In an unguarded
moment he had revealed to the Indians that his pay
was one peso a day; and the next morning in his place
there came Juan Tomas', the old war chief, and Chico
Romero, the young tribal chief. If there was any easy
money in sight they figured it was their legitimate
graft, and it was much easier to tell a few stories than
to shell five gallons of oyster meat.

Far from feeling any shame over his theft of a piece
of canvas, Juan Tomas' entered the tent with a swag-
ger and told Hampton that *he* would talk. He would
sing a war song, in the original old Seri, now forgotten by all but him; and his nephew, Chico Romero,
would interpret it into Spanish. This, however, was
just a device to get Chico on the pay roll, as his Spanish was very limited.

He was a big, goofy man, who still retained his
baby name of Won't Suck; and, in the eyes of the
Seris, he was not even a chief, having been appointed
to his position by the Government Agent, who wanted
a man he could handle. Juan Tomas' still wore about
his neck the paper, signed by the Governor of Sonora,
officially acknowledging his authority, but in this case
they stood together to make the Yoris pay. Hampton
recognized the situation at a glance, but it was part of
his system to placate the ruling chiefs. For if anything

was done to offend them, they were capable of serious mischief.

So Juan Tomas' sat on one box, across the table, with Chico Romero on another; and, in order to deal with these troublemakers, Big Beard was called in to make the record. A sheaf of paper was laid out, he poised his fountain-pen, and the ancient war song began. In a low, almost inaudible voice, Juan Tomas' sang it through to the end. It took him forty minutes and then he began all over again, translating it into modern Seri for the benefit of Chico Romero. That took forty minutes more, and not a word had been written down. For the third time he went back to the beginning; but, the moment Chico began to interpret, an old woman broke in and corrected him.

Under the matriarchal form of government which prevails among the Seris the women consider themselves as good as the men-folks if not a little better. They spoke right up in meeting, and Juan Tomas' was soon completely cowed. He finally subsided into sullen silence and let them argue it out. Then he began all over again, while Chico tried to turn it into Spanish.

It was a battle from the start, with a milling crowd of Indians looking on, and Americano made it more confusing by trying to get the old Seri words. In his youth he had once served under a trained anthropologist—a man who measured his Indians in millimeters and recorded their words in Government script—and that was his fixed idea of what we ought to want. But what we really wanted was just the opposite—the Indian songs, translated literally into English, with nothing added and nothing left out. This, however,

was not the time nor the place to argue the point, so
we let him have his way.

Here is the song, just as it came, with incredible
labor, through three languages and then into English.
But first the original old Seri:

Tay sah may nay
Tay sah may nay
Ah way ah say
Ah say kai yay.

Kai yah, kai yah!

This refrain ran off into a muttered grumble and
every verse was the same, except that a few words
were added. One verse is as good as a thousand. It
meant nothing, even to the Seris; but was like an ancient litany which, once started, had to be chanted
through to the end.

The Old Song—*Eee-go'-set*—which follows—was
said by Juan Tomas' to be very old: "This song came
down from seven grandfathers. It was taught one to
another. In the old days this song was given only to a
brave man's son. The language is not that of the Modern Seris but is an ancient language which could not
be communicated by words. It is very old."

Neither Chico nor Old Tomas' knew who this big
man was; but he was a giant, a terrible warrior, and
the man who killed him was a war chief. It is a war
song and makes men strong and brave in battle.

Eee-go'-set

I am in my house—a cave—alone.
Outside there is a great disturbance.

I want to know what is happening.
I hear a great noise of the thunder
And with my very long bow
I shoot an arrow at a giant cactus.
It blows up like lightning—
Blows up and falls.

When I go outside I inquire
Why is all this disturbance.
And they are angry
And frightened,
And they want to fight me.
When I come outside of my cave
I tell these people to keep quiet.
And again they are angry.

When I come outside I tell them
I cannot sleep. Only a woman can sleep.
The ants are biting me and keeping me awake
And I want quiet.
If I can't sleep I will take my weapons—
Bows and arrows, with my quiver,
My best breastplate of stone,
And my back-plate of stone,
And I will go forth to fight my enemies.
Therefore I go forth with my arms.
I hunt the trail of one who comes,
Hidden by a dry giant cactus.

He comes with his head so high
It is in the sky.
His hat is so high
It is like a cloud.
His eyes are so high

That he cannot see me on earth.
He is angry when he cannot find me
And he pulls his mustache,
He is so angry
Because he cannot find me.
His head is so high
That when he looks to the ground
He cannot see me.

The Tall One is so brave
And the Tall One is so strong
That I sit down in fear
Behind a dry ironwood.
I load my medicine pipe
It is so very large;
And with a dry stick, twirling,
I make fire, to light my pipe.
And I quit smoking, afraid.
The tears run down my cheeks
Because I am afraid.

The medicine has worked.
I throw my pipe aside.
Now there has been enough smoking.
I pull down my quiver
And I challenge him
To fight a combat with ten arrows
To see who is the braver man.
I shout to him:
"I will plant an arrow in your throat."
And he draws his bow to fight.

I shoot an arrow through him
From side to side,

But he is not dead.
He says: "Do not kill me—
I won't fight any more."
I grab his great bow
And smash his head
But he is not dead.

I chop off his head
And make a hole in his cheek
And drag his great head
To the people who made so much noise
That I could not sleep.
They see I am very brave
And they dance for a long time
Before my house.

It was almost unbelievable, under the circumstances, but before they got through Juan Tomas' and Chico Romero had given us a very good song. A song which showed by internal evidence that the Seris had not always been savages. There had been a time, dating back through the lives of seven grandfathers, when, instead of being Pre-Stone Age in their culture, they had fashioned stone breastplates and worn them.

In the Hozoni Chant of the Navajos, describing the destruction of Pueblo Bonito, there are frequent references to the Flint Boys—men clothed in armor made of flint or iron, the word *besh* being used for both. There are also, in their sand-paintings, pictures of Nahyenesgani, the War God and his brother, Tobaadzizini, attired from head to foot in bristling armor. This was either metal armor, brought by their ancestors from Asia, or stone armor made in this country. But the later Navajo warriors fought stripped to the waist, wearing a heavy robe of buckskin wrapped around their bellies to protect them from enemy arrows.

Armor made of wooden slats was used in British Columbia, cotton armor was worn in Mexico and Peru, and overlapping plates of ivory and bone have been found along the North Pacific Coast. But this reference to

> My best breastplate of stone
> And my back-plate of stone

seems to indicate a higher grade of culture than the present-day Seris possess. Since they do not even shape their stone implements now, they have been rated by McGee as Pre-Stone Age.

At a much later date, when the Seris fought only with jagged beach-stones called *ahst*, they wore armor down to their knees made from sea-lion skin. On top of this, they tied flat stones over their chests—and sometimes one on each side of the head. The only place where an arrow could wound them was in the upper part of the face. This helmet was decorated with long plumes made of crow-feathers—two long ones underneath and then shorter ones on top, reaching out behind and separating the two stones.

This, and much more, we learned later from Santo Blanco; but now Juan Tomas' held the stage. He was a tall, wrinkled old man, claiming to be one hundred and three years old—not because he could count that much but because he could remember when Hermosillo did not exist, and other events which indicated extreme age. When he was a boy a feud broke out between his family and another family and they went out to kill one of these men; but in the battle all three of his brothers were killed and Juan got a bullet through his left hand, so that he could not hold a bow to shoot. He was waiting for his hand to heal and grow strong when he got hold of an old cap-and-ball musket and immediately shot the man who had killed them.

Thus, early in life, he had acquired a reputation as a killer and the Seris were deathly afraid of him. His little red eyes had the look of a ferret's, and his deformed left hand was always there to remind them that in war he was inexorable. He seems to have come from a different breed of Indians, his short hair being distinctly curly; and he was the only man among them who had blue lines tattooed down his chin.

On the second day he entered the tent with his head held high, but during the night there had been a division among the people regarding Chico's ability as an interpreter, and a quarrel began at once. It was finally decided that Martin Villalobo should take Chico's place, and *Eee-go'-set* should be done all over again. So the old chief sat down and, in a voice barely audible, sang the whole song over again—forty minutes! Since nobody could understand the ancient words, not a voice had been raised in protest; but when, in Modern Seri, he repeated it to Martin, a hot argument sprang up which our interpreter was unable to stop.

As far as we were concerned *Eee-go'-set* was finished, but with them it had just begun. And Americano declared that the ancient words had to be written down all over again:

Mose-nik quee-kose

Hah-pay may say
Poo' kai quee mo ick'
Ah no kay' say puu-wick'.

And so on for an hour, until we called a halt. It was all very interesting—with a rhythm and apparently a rhyme—but what we wanted was the English words. Something we could understand. So at last we began all over again—and the song was barely recognizable.

Ee-go'-set—Old Song
(as interpreted by Martín Villalobo)

The song says this:

A man is in his house—a large cave—alone.
The outside is strewn with the bones
Of the people the Seris have killed.
Their heads are white.

I am the only great man among these people.
All others are like women.
I go out of my house
And I am looking from side to side
For a great, dry cactus.

I see a big man coming towards me,
Big as a giant cactus.
He is so tall his head reaches the sky.
His sombrero is so big that twenty men cannot
    lift it.
His eyes are seven yards apart.

His mouth is full of great teeth with holes in
    them,
And when he breathes they go out and in with
    his breath.
He had an arrow as big as the arc of your hands.
When he planted his bow on the ground
Thunder broke in the sky.

The two came together and sat down.
They smoked out of the giant's pipe.
The giant took a stick from the fire and said:
"Press this against my forehead
And I will stand it until it goes out."

The Seri said: "We will see who is the best man."
He pulled his quiver down and shot one arrow.
It struck the giant in his right side
And came out on the left.
He fell over.

I mashed his head with his bow and he fell dead.
I cut off his head and dragged it home
By a hole I cut in his cheek.

Here ended, with much sound and fury, the second version—or rather, interpretation—of the ancient war song; and, while the Indians were all talking at once, a girl reached over and laid a piece of paper on the table. It was Ramona, the only Seri woman who had been to school; and on the paper, in Spanish, she had written the words of a song. Hampton snatched it up, asked her a question in Spanish, then grabbed a peso from his pocket and slammed it down on the table.

"What's that for?" I asked, and in great excitement he said:

"To pay her for that song—the first Seri song ever written down by an Indian!"

"But what good is it to you?" I inquired. "And why did you pay her so much?"

"Well," he admitted, a little abashed. "I made a mistake and gave her the peso instead of a two-cent piece."

It certainly was a mistake, as far as the Indians were concerned. Ramona begged some paper and began to write more, Hampton refused to buy them and she passed them on to me. When I refused them the poor girl was bewildered—but anyhow, she had her peso.

We began again in the afternoon, and at my request Hampton asked the other Indians to leave—all except the ones who were reciting. That quieted things down, Chico Romero resumed his post, and went ahead with the Balsa Song. A balsa is a raft-boat, made of bundles of *carrizo* bamboo bound together, and the story is the continuation of the adventures of the war chief, after he had returned from slaying the giant. He had gone a long way to meet the giant, and it was a long journey in his balsa home. He was tired and lay down to sleep, and this song came to him like a dream.

BALSA SONG

I am paddling my balsa over the waters
Which are everywhere
And I paddle for two days till sleep comes.
Sleep comes and I dream
And in the dream comes this song.

While I am asleep on my balsa
I am so tired I want to anchor.
I can paddle no more.
But I have no rock (to tie to)
I put my line in the water—
It is of mesquite roots—
And it goes about the neck of a turtle
Which is my anchor.
And to me this song comes.

The turtle says he is tired and hungry
And it tells him, while I sleep,
To go to the shore where he will find food.
But the Cahuama says:
"I must go where there is seaweed to eat."
And, while I sleep, he takes me far out to sea.

I dreamed I saw a black-tail deer
So I went to hunt.
I wandered across the desert
And found a deer lying down.
But he was very watchful.
He turned his head from side to side
While he looked for me.
But he did not see me.
He was suspicious and jumped up
And ran away, before I could kill him.

I dreamed that a man died
And he lay out straight
But he was not buried.
He was killed by the soldiers
So he lay there for two days.

He did not wish to die
But wished to go on his road.
But he was dead two days
So he could not follow the road,
With nothing but his bones.

   This grim joke brought a laugh from the people
outside, who were listening through the entrance, and
Juan Tomas' was encouraged to go on. But this time,
instead of a *cancion*, or song, he gave us a *cuenta*, or
story.

A man went forth from a cave, because he had no meat to eat. But all around him were clams—many, many clams, with piles of shells where people had eaten for so long. And the piles of shell were very big.

The man went out from the cave, hunting for the being who gave them food to eat—a man whose food was people. And he hunted a long time.

The next day he came back and all the people were very sad. Because he did not bring a deer or a cow or a pig or a horse, and they told him to hunt some more.

So the man went out a third time, and he was sad because he had found nothing for his people to eat. After hunting a long time he came to a tall tree which made a good shade, and he sat down to rest.

He rested and then he stood up, but he did not walk —he only listened. And he heard a sound and, though he looked all around him, he could not find the people who made these sounds.

He said: "Who can this be?" and listened again. He heard a crow sing and he was frightened and thought it was people. He did not know it was a crow.

He came to a house and in this lived a chief of the "Old People," before the Seris, called *Sais-koh'-shet*. One half of these people would eat meat of the cow and one half would not; but they would eat fish from the sea, such as sharks or porpoise or turtles. So he got into a big balsa and went over on the south side of the Island.

That was the end of this simple tale and, after thinking a while, Juan Tomas' began another tale, called *Col-qui''-e-net*. It is all dreams that a man has —a very primitive folk story.

The Buzzard

In the old days, Zopilote, the buzzard, was a man—
and his wives were twenty. He went out into the
mountains to look for food and found a dead black-tail
deer. Zopilote lived on the big sand-hill before you
come to the rock near Tiburon, where there is a great
deal of clam shell. He went out again to look for food
where there were many sharks, but the sharks had
driven away the fish and he could get no food. So,
when he came back, his wives were hungry.

Again he went out to hunt, to a far place near the
Island, and while he was gone his wife, Calele, the
scavenger-hawk, stole his bow and arrows and hid
them in the brush, because she knew another man was
coming. While Zopilote was returning without game
he was very thoughtful and he said to himself:

"Why do I have such bad luck? Twice I have gone
out and got nothing."

When he was coming back he came slowly, and he
looked toward his house on the high sand-hill and he
saw that all his family were lying around the house,
killed. He watched before he landed and then sneaked
through the brush to his house. But everybody was
dead. Only one wife was left in the house—she who
had hidden his bow and arrows. So he took his spear,
which was with him while he was hunting, and said to
his wife:

"Why are all these people killed? And who has hidden my bow and arrows?" He told her to bring them
back and she did.

He took his bow and arrows and followed the trail
of the bad one, and the bad one went north through

the brush, where the trail was very crooked. He said
to the trail:

"Where did this bad one go?"
The Trail said:

"Follow along to where the trail turns east."
And behind him came all the birds and animals—because then all birds and animals were Seris.

The crow cut off all his hair, from the back of his
neck over his head like a scalp, and tied it to a stick
which he carried over his shoulder, and everybody
was happy. They danced and sang as they followed
the Zopilote. They found the bad one asleep beside
the trail in the shade of a bush. So all the followers together killed him. Zopilote returned to his house,
where his wife was waiting for him. He said:

"Let us go on a journey."

He went to the north to a far-off place now called
Tepopa and said to his wife:

"I have hunted and found nothing. You go back
and find animals to eat. I will never hunt again. You
find dead animals and send back word to us, the other
birds."

He flew up into the sky, where he could watch
them, and the young people looked down at the tracks
and said:

"What tracks are those?"

"Look well," he said. He pointed down at the tracks
and said: "That is *Nahl*."

So the children all learned to call the Calele woman
Nahl, and when they became men they only knew this
one by that name. This is so ancient that it was before
the Seris became men.

CHAPTER VI

Santo Blanco Takes Over

IT WAS evident that Juan Tomas' was running out
of stories. From his ancient war song, a classic of
its kind, he had descended to a series of folk stories,
and very poor ones at that. Several times before, in
working with other tribes, we had noticed how dull
and ignorant the warrior class can be. They could ter-
rorize the medicine men by their overbearing ways,
but of the intellectual life of the people they knew almost nothing.

For a peso a day, Juan Tomas' had been quick to
pre-empt the job of historian; but when, during the
night, a truckload of liquor came in, he was just as
quick to drop it. There was money in camp now, for
the bass had begun to bite, and the bootleggers came
rushing in. All the able-bodied Seris were making
money but, before their women could get the price of
a dress, the men had gone on a drunk.

The next morning Juan Tomas' did not return, and
I talked with Mr. Corona. He knew and I knew that
nobody else would dare to take the war chief's job;
but all along I had had my eye on Santo Blanco, the
chief medicine man of the tribe. For four nights, for
the good of his people, he had been singing his songs
of praise to every fish in the sea; and every morning I
had been feeding him and giving him coffee. He would
be so worn out and tired he could hardly move; but,
after a hearty breakfast, he would rise up silently and
go off down the trail for more oysters.

Though the Seris knew he had a family to support, no one showed him the slightest compassion; and yet he had brought the fish. On the second day of the Fish Chant, two enormous sea bass had been caught; and on the third day, eleven more. There was feasting and singing in the Seri camp—and on the fourth day the bass were running strong. Over the side of the boat they could be seen in the depths, gliding in shoals as they moved up the Gulf toward their feeding grounds farther north. Every fishing boat at Kino Bay was out at daylight, but still Santo Blanco went hungry. Either he caught no fish or he liked our food better, and Angelito had orders to feed him. Perhaps Santo Blanco had understood from the start that I liked him and wanted him to talk. But when I mentioned him to Corona he dismissed him with a word.

"All he thinks about is money!" he exclaimed contemptuously.

"Well, is that so bad?" I asked. "If a man loves money he is easy to handle. All you have to do is pay him."

"Yes, and the minute he finds out that you want his stuff, the price will go up and up!"

"All the same," I said, "I want him. But what about Juan Tomas'?"

"If he makes you any trouble," said Corona, "just report the matter to me. The ground on which your tent stands is part of my concession, and I have authority from the Governor of Sonora to put every Indian off."

Mr. Corona had no fear of the Indians, and I knew he was man enough to protect me, so I engaged Santo Blanco. But, in order not to spoil him at the start— and get him in wrong with Juan Tomas'—I gave him only one peso a day. He took the place of two men, and filled both of them better, but if I paid him more it would start another war. What the two chiefs were waiting for was just this—to have me hire another man. Then they would make me pay tribute or scare him away.

Santo Blanco came into the office tent very quietly, a little scared of Juan Tomas' but hating Chico Romero, whose brother had stolen his daughter Ramona; and we had scarcely got down to work when the war chiefs came barging in.

"Please tell Juan Tomas'," I said to Americano, "that Santo Blanco is working for me now, and I must ask him to keep quiet."

Juan Tomas' had been drinking and his eyes were dangerous, but Santo Blanco never flinched. Most of the Seris backed out of the door, but he remained where he was.

"No!" said Juan Tomas'.

"Tell him," I went on, "that when he was singing his songs for me I asked everybody to keep quiet. I want to get the songs of the Seris right—and, when I ask him to sing for me again, I will tell everybody to go."

This put a different color on the request and, after thinking it over, he thrust out his hand and roared:

"*Da me cigarros!*"

I handed him one, and he shouted louder. Then I gave him the whole pack and, having saved his face, he went away. The rest of the crowd followed, Red Hat closed the flaps and we settled down to record the Fish Chant.

Santo Blanco is a sturdy little shock-headed man with a subdued intensity in his mild, black eyes and a

When the fish began to bite—plenty for all.

(Photograph by Dane Coolidge)

Santo Blanco, wearing his medicine man's crown, sings a song to the whale, chief of the fishes. (Photograph by Dane Coolidge)

very melodious voice. He leaned on the table, tapping out the rhythm with his finger; then, in the low tone which all the Seris use, he began on the Whale Song. It is the first of the hundreds of songs sung to every fish that lives in the sea—for the whale is that Great Chief of Fishes, the *Capitan* to which they pray. I was afire to get this chant down as soon as possible, before somebody else interfered; but Americano held up everything while he wrote out the Seri words.

Ah kain' qui ko'-ait. The Whale Song.

He wrote it down slowly, repeating the spelling to me; but his spelling was intended for Spanish-speaking people—I wanted mine in English. *Qui* in Spanish is the same as "kee" in English, but Hampton insisted on *qui*. He was a very good interpreter, a master of the Spanish language; so I let it go as *qui*. Then at last I got:

The Whale Song

The whale is swimming
Back and forth in the water.
He drinks very much water
And he goes here and there,
And here and there.
He comes to me
At the edge of the land.

The ballad gives a very impressive picture of the huge mammal which they look upon as the Chief of the Fishes, coming up to the edge of the land in answer to this song. Seeing it spout vapor when it comes to the surface, the Seris think it has been drinking water and is spouting water. The whale looms big in the life of these Indians as, from their camps along

El Infiernillo, they could look out into Rada Ballena and see the great animals at play. At a later time I got this truly magnificent poem, or series of poems describing their life and death.

THE SONG OF THE WHALE

I am large and very strong.
I am swift through the water.
Because of my speed I fear nothing.
No shark can catch me.

The sea is calm
There is no wind.
In the warm sun
I play on the surface
With many companions.
In the air spout
Many clouds of smoke
And all of them are happy.

The mother whale is happy.
She swims on the surface, very fast.
No shark is near
But she swims over many leagues
Back and forth, very fast.
Then she sinks to the bottom
And four baby whales are born.

First one comes up to the surface
In front of her nose.
He jumps on the surface.
Then each of the other baby whales
Jumps on the surface.

Then they go down
Into the deep water to their mother
And stay there eight days
Before they come up again.

The old, old whale has no children.
She does not swim far.
She floats near the shore and is sad.
She is so old and weak
She cannot feed like other whales.
With her mouth on the surface
She draws in her breath—hrrr—
And the smallest fish and the sea birds are swal-
    lowed up.

The whale coming to shore is sick
The sharks have eaten her bowels
And the meat of her body.
She travels slowly—her bowels are gone.
She is dead on the shore
And can travel no longer.

Fifty sharks surrounded her.
They came under her belly
And bit off her flesh and her bowels
And so she died. Because she had no teeth
To fight the sharks.

Perhaps it was a premonition of the beautiful songs
yet to come which made me so impatient with John
Hampton. I had told him several times that I did not
want the Seri words, even refusing to write them
down; but still, at the ponderous pace of a stone-
crusher, he insisted upon recording the titles in the

Seri language. And Santo Blanco quite entered into the spirit of his research, repeating the words over and over while Hampton dictated the spelling. It took an eternity, as he wrote very slowly—and at last I called a halt.

"What is the use," I asked, "of your writing it down, when I have a copy, already?"

"Why," he explained, in genuine astonishment, though he had never mentioned it before, "I intend to use this myself, in my vocabulary of the Seri language."

"All right," I responded, "if you think there is any demand for it. But please don't hold up the story—what I want is this series of Fish Songs."

"Very well," he replied, throwing down his pencil impatiently, and I signaled Santo Blanco to proceed. He leaned against the table, gazing into space as he hummed his next song in Seri. Then, in his careful Spanish, he repeated the words to Hampton and he in turn interpreted them to me. It took only a few minutes, if we left out the linguistics, and celebrated the *Tortuava*, a large fish, something like a porpoise.

THE TORTUAVA SONG

The tortuava drinks
A great deal of salt water
Until he is like a drunkard.
And he rolls back and forth in the water
As he comes to me
On the edge of the land.

It was the second in the series of three or four hundred, and a very sophisticated form of verse for a savage. The comparison to a drunkard was an apt

simile and I was eager to go ahead, when Hampton
held everything up again. I could not understand this
sudden enthusiasm for the making of a Seri vocabulary. If the words were recorded in the special al-
phabet which anthropologists use they might have a
certain value, but John was a botanist and not quali-
fied for such technical work. And yet, laboriously,
while I waited, he was writing down the Seri text.

Once more my impatience overcame me and I
asked him why he was recording them, when they
were of no use whatever to me.

"Why," he responded, "I am getting them for myself. I am going to write a book on the Seris."

This was news to me and very bad news, for I
would consider myself lucky if my own book ever appeared in print, and there was hardly room for two
books. But if, on top of that, he intended to use the
time which I was paying him for, to collate a Seri
dictionary, our arrangement could not go on.

"All right," I said. "We quit right here, and I will
get me another interpreter."

I gave Santo Blanco his peso and went out to take
some photographs, and when I returned I found
Hampton in a more subdued state of mind. He had not
understood, he said, that it would be unethical for
him to use my time to obtain material for his book;
but if we thought so, he would consider staying on.
Especially as I would find it very difficult to get a com-
petent interpreter.

He was, of course, the best man in the country for
this purpose, as he understood the peculiar, broken
Spanish by which the Seris turned their verbs into
gerunds, saying "running" instead of ran or run, so
at last it was agreed. There was no great institution

behind us and we were spending our own money—
trying to make it a carefree adventure, though done
with as much fidelity as was possible. But we had engaged him, not to direct the research, but to guide us
into the country and keep us from getting killed.

Looking back over our journey from the Border—
which had taken ten days where it could have been
made in three or four—we could see that only con-
fusion had resulted from divided leadership, so I suggested to Americano that I would take over the management myself. Then Red Hat, who had been rather
overlooked in the misunderstanding, assumed the role
of peacemaker and finally everything was smoothed
out. Americano agreed to confine himself to botany
when not engaged in interpreting, and to leave the
direction of the expedition to us.

Meanwhile a violent *barullo* had sprung up in the
Indian village and, when a messenger came running
to summon Hampton, we drove over there to watch
the fight.

CHAPTER VII

No Law At Kino Bay

THERE was no law of any kind at Kino Bay. The fishermen paid no licenses to the Federal Government, and stayed ashore when they sighted the Fish Patrol. They dynamited the bass when they would not bite, and there was no one to say them nay. The amiable Mr. Corona was fully occupied in attending to his own business and, but for the bootleggers, all would have been well.

Corona himself was bitterly opposed to selling liquor to the Indians. What they needed was clothes and food, and material to mend their old, broken-down boats, which could hardly be kept afloat. But, twenty-four hours after the fish began to run, the mezcal peddlers drifted in.

Chico Romero was the first to get drunk, and then old, red-eyed Tomas'; and, with them to set the example, the rest could not be restrained. Up at the shed where the fish were weighed, a piratical-looking Greek named Pedro was buying the sea bass as they were brought in. The Americans and Mexicans sold theirs by the kilo; but when the Seris staggered in with their catch they received seventy-five centavos apiece for the small ones, and a peso apiece for the large ones. Santo Blanco complained that that was *muy barrato*, very cheap; especially as, to Pedro's beady eyes, practically all the Seris' fish looked small. But, as Corona had explained before, "all he thought about was money."

73

Having received his peso from us, Santo Blanco was now pushing his boat into the water to go out and catch some fish. He had a wife and eight daughters to provide for and could not stop to get drunk. The others, however, were troubled by no such scruples, and as we drove up to the Ugarte house, near their village, there were *borrachos* everywhere. Mrs. Ugarte, who lived there and handed out the mezcal, was a respectable, hard-working woman who would do all the laundry we could bring her for a peso.

She certainly was not getting much of a cut on this bootlegging or she would not need to work at all, but somebody was making a good thing of it at twenty centavos a drink, and it was probably her son. This Ramon Ugarte was a tall young Spaniard, who also bought fish from the Indians, and Corona gave him a bad name. He was bold and defiant, always wore an automatic pistol and had no fear at all of the Seris, as we soon found out.

About a month before, Ramon had come to Corona and told him that the Indians owed him money, and he wanted him to help collect it. He then went to nine Seris who had receipts for fish bought by Corona, and told them if they would give him the papers he would collect their money for them. Then he requested the fish merchant to give him one receipt for the nine, and to make it out in his name. But when Corona paid the bill, Ramon kept all the money, although the Indians threatened to kill him.

Now that the sea bass were beginning to run again and the Seris wanted money to buy liquor, Ramon had bought more fish; but his truck had not come in time and they were beginning to spoil. That made no great difference to the Seris, who do not mind eating

old fish; but, when Ramon refused to honor the receipts
he had given them, they tried to get their fish back.
But Ugarte would not allow it. They returned in force
and tore down part of his fence before he could drive
them away. Now the great *barullo* was on—one man
against the whole tribe.

Juan Tomas' had lined up all his warriors and, with
a skinful of Ramon's own poisonous liquor, was orat-
ing and calling for a charge. The Mexican Government had given Chico Romero three Mauser rifles for
their protection, and he was passing around the cartridges when Americano appeared on the scene. He
arrived in great excitement, as he had been told the
fight was on and the Indians were about to burn the
houses down.

But, when he got there, Ugarte was calmly await-
ing the charge. There was still time to avert the battle
and Hampton rushed out to intercede with the warriors. He counseled them one and all not to fight, but
to send their chie ᴜ Hermosillo to report the affair to
the Government. This was just what the Seris had
been waiting for as young Ramon was known to be a
dead shot and h ad shown no intention of yielding.
So they turned the matter over to Chico Romero and
nothing ever came of it.

Early in the day Chico had got a shot of bad liquor,
which made his head wag back and forth like that of a
man with the palsy, and he was in no condition to call
on the Governor and make a demand for protection.
If he had, the request would undoubtedly have been
granted, as the Mexican Government is greatly concerned for the welfare of its Indians. Only a few days
later a Seri came into camp with his feet full of cactus
thorns and reported that, of nine Seris in a house at

Punta Coyote, he alone had escaped alive. During the night some Mexican fishermen with whom they had had trouble had slipped up and thrown dynamite among them. He had been outside at the time, but he had seen the explosion and, as far as he knew, all the people in the house had been killed.

This was sad news for Manuel Encinas and his wife, for they had three sons at Punta Coyote and did not know whether they were alive or dead. Yet the old man was afraid to go up there, lest the Mexicans should kill him, also. But, though drunken Chico did nothing, two days later a troop of Mexican cavalry was seen from Tiburon, riding north to the scene of the attack. Yet, six weeks later, Manuel was still waiting to learn the fate of his sons.

To be sure the Seris had a *Jefe de Vigilancia*, a Government Agent, who was supposed to be their protector and friend; but, unless everybody at Kino Bay was lying, he was giving the bootleggers a free hand. He it was who had had Chico appointed chief, though the people did not approve of him. Every time Romero started for Hermosillo to lay their grievances before the Government he got drunk before he reached the Capitol, and the Government knew nothing about it.

That something was wrong at Kino Bay we knew before the end of the day. A fishing boat from Guaymas had anchored off the village and the crew, besides supplying the natives with liquor, had taken aboard an Indian prostitute. She was a wild-looking creature and now, crazy with drink, she was singing and screaming boisterously. The *Jefe de Vigilancia* was there on the beach when the bootleggers put her ashore, but he did not interfere. As for the Seris, they looked on in silence—there was no law at Kino Bay.

These two *barullos* left the village in a tumult, and the drinking continued all night; but the next morning Santo Blanco, a little bleary-eyed, appeared for breakfast. He was especially fond of hot rice, served with syrup made from melting down *panoches* of raw sugar, and he was sitting by the fire scooping it up with a big spoon when Americano appeared. It was a week since I had begun to make a pet out of Santo Blanco by giving him a big breakfast but, as Hampton was a very late sleeper, he had not been aware of the fact. So, when he beheld our medicine man, it gave him quite a shock.

"What?" he said. "Feeding Indians in camp?"

"Sure," I replied. "We need him in our business. I've been feeding him every morning for a week."

"Well!" he exclaimed, looking Santo Blanco over, "if you want to eat with an Indian you can. I'll have my breakfast in my tent."

He poured out a cup of coffee and went away, and Angelito looked scared. On account of the multiplicity of *barullos* in our midst I had not got around to tell him that we had had a change of management, but as Santo Blanco slipped away I tried my halting Spanish on our *mozo*.

We had picked him up at Costa Rica Ranch, where he had been raising beans on shares. But a long-continued fog had mildewed the crop and he had been glad to come along as cook. Angelito Coronado was his name and he was a blue-eyed Mexican. We found out later he was a Mayo Indian, over half of the tribe having blue eyes and yellow hair or other signs of Nordic blood. The Mayos have a story that, long before Cortez and the Spaniards came, a crippled ship sailed up the Mayo River from the sea. The people in it settled among the Mayos, teaching them many things, including such Norse words as *brot* for bread.

They are a superior tribe of Indians, the majority having light complexions, whereas their Yaqui neighbors and kinsmen are almost black. The men are broad-shouldered and sturdy, the women full-breasted and tall; and the tribe has produced some great military leaders. The most famous was General Al'varo Obregon, who later became President of Mexico. On account of his twinkling blue eyes, the Irish soldiers of fortune used to claim he was an O'Brien; but his lineage goes back to the *ancestors* of the fighting Irish, the Norse pirates who swept down from the north.

Angelito was small and not of the soldier type, but he was absolutely dependable; and often in the evening we would try out our Spanish on him, though Hampton did not approve. Having spent so many years in the Latin-American countries, he had taken on the ways of the upper classes, to whom a servant is something less than the dust. But Angelito was a free man, and a good one, and we refused to treat him like a peon. Americano had become more or less accustomed to that, but when he saw this lousy Indian, Santo Blanco, with his dirty feet to the fire, eating rice out of his favorite white plate, it was more than he could bear.

"Angelito," I began, when Hampton had disappeared, "no more now is Americano *patron*. I am *patron!*" and I tapped myself on the chest. "El Americano lives now as our priest. But I am boss. When you want anything—talk to me."

" '*Sta bueno!*" responded Angelito; and asked about the feed for his horse. Buro Alazan had been cutting grass for it with a butcher knife, and I told him to

keep right on paying him with his breakfast—as he
had been doing, surreptitiously, all the time. Then I
asked him how much Americano had agreed to pay
him. He shrugged—there had been no agreement—
but he had hoped to receive two pesos a day. I told
him I was sorry, but I had heard Jim Blevins, the
rancher at Costa Rica, tell Hampton, on no account to
pay him over one—and he was getting his board besides.

This left poor Angelito feeling very sad, for he had
a wife and four children to provide for; but when I
asked him if a peso and a half would be enough, the
old happy smile came back. That was the official wage
for laborers, as recently declared by the Mexican Government; but no one was paying it yet and Blevins did
not want us to begin. At the same time Angelito was
a faithful worker, remaining in camp twenty-four
hours a day to keep the Indians out, and we wanted
to have him satisfied. I told him further that, when
any of his friends dropped in, he was welcome to give
them coffee and something to eat.

That was one custom of the country which Hampton had consistently ignored. When we were camped
at the abandoned ranch a band of vaqueros had waited
around for an hour in the hope of getting a cup of
coffee, and had ridden away unfed. Now we were
starting all over again, and Angelito seemed more
pleased with this than he was in receiving a raise.
That afternoon I gave him half a day off, to go up and
visit the Lodge, which made him still more happy.

As our guest Hampton suddenly changed his ways
and, as if by magic, everything straightened out and
we went ahead writing down songs. Just the English
words from the Spanish—no pottering around to get

the Seri original—and at first Santo Blanco was per-
plexed. All the other Americans who had come to
Kino Bay had been interested in linguistics and he
kept on repeating the Seri words; but I refused to
write them down and at last we began where we had
left off, with the Sea Turtle Song.

THE TURTLE SONG:

The *cahuama* swims on top
Where there is no wind.
When the wind blows he goes down
On the bottom for a long time.
When the wind stops he travels far
Looking for food,
And he eats the seaweed.

THE CANOE SONG:

When the wind blows I don't go out
Into the open sea,
And sometimes for four or five days
I don't have to work.

THE WIND SONG (sung very slowly)

The wind begins
Far off in the sea.
And it blows cold,
Over here and all over the monte (brush-land).

THE CACTUS FRUIT SONG:

The pitahaya is now ripe
And I am glad.
When I went out to look
The cactus was in flower
And gave me nothing to eat.

THE SONG OF THE BLACK-TAIL DEER:

When the sun shines the *buro* is hot
And, with his companions,
He looks for shade under the trees.
He lies down under a palo verde tree
And his companions lie down a little way off
Under the shade of other trees.

North of Kino Bay there is a big mountain where
the Seris have a sacred cave.

THE BIG MOUNTAIN SONG:

I am sad because it has not rained.
All my trees and brush are dying.
Because it does not rain
Many of my trees are dead.

The sacred cave is occupied by a spirit—white like
a Gringo.

THE CAVE SONG:

To the big cave in the mountain
He comes from the daylight;
And he sits, smoking his pipe, in the darkness.
With his hand on his breast he sits all night
When the cave is light, like day.
In the day the cave is dark.
In the night the cave is light.

This spirit who comes is like a god of the White
People. He has a round black hat, black robes and,
underneath, a white skirt.

Song of the Winds:

Below the sea there is the mouth of a cave
In which all the winds are born.
He comes below the sea and mounts up
To where there is no sun.
But the cave is light, like the sun.

Another mouth is smooth and slippery
And hard, like ice.
He stands erect with his arms outstretched
And from each finger there comes a wind.

First he blows the White Wind
Then he blows the Red Wind
Then he blows the Blue Wind.
And from his little finger
He blows the Black Wind,
Which is stronger than them all.

The White Wind comes from the north
And is very hot.
Blue comes from the south.
The Red Wind comes from the west
In the middle of the day, and is soft.
The Black Wind comes from beyond the moun-
    tains
And is strongest of them all.
The Whirlwind comes from the east.

The Wind God makes them come
From the points of his fingers—
White from his first
Red from his second
Blue from his third
Black from his fourth.

Here was the first touch of a formal religion that
we had encountered—the first indication that the
Seris had gods. Or were descended from a people who
had gods. This Wind God who dwelt in a cave and
sent forth good and bad winds was strikingly similar
to the Greek god Aeolus, and the other Wind Gods of
mythology. Was the Seri Wind God a mere coin-
cidence, or had we touched the fringe of a greater
pantheon, which would connect them with world-wide
beliefs?

While I was meditating on this, Santo Blanco began
to sing, tapping out the time with his finger as he
hummed:

THE WIND GOD'S MARRIAGE:

The Wind God sang a song
And went from his house.
He went among the trees
And sang the song again.

Then a woman came to meet him
With her arms outstretched.
And in each hand,
She carried flowers.

He brought her no presents—
No meat, no food, no clothes.
But they were wed
And she sat beside him
And he took her hand in his.

How many Greek and Latin poets have celebrated
the loves of the gods! But few of them more beauti-

fully than this ragged little Santo Blanco—and he had a mythology of his own! Handed down through the ages in these soft-toned songs, from a time when the Seris were not barbarians.

CHAPTER VIII

About God and the Ancient Ways

I COULD have hugged Santo Blanco, the way Hampton had embraced Juan Tomas'; but, remembering what had come from that, I gave him his peso and said nothing. I knew now that the Seris had a definite mythology and, if I kept my face straight and restrained my enthusiasm, my little friend would reveal it. He could see that I was pleased with his songs —and I told him they were good; but the next morning I let him begin where he would, without asking him for more.

He was a medicine man and I knew that, sooner or later, he would get back to the gods. His first three songs had been poems of nature, personifying natural objects in the true, pantheistic way. He even sang in the person of the mountain or a canoe, and he went on with more and more of the same type.

THE SARDINE SONG:

I swim and swim
The water comes very cold.
If I do not swim far
In this cold water
I will die.

I swim very far
To the man who sings this song
And do not die.

85

THE BALSA SONG:
(Sung by the balsa, a boat-like raft, made of canes)

I go a long journey with a tired hunter.
He is so tired he cannot spear any turtles.
He cannot kill any food.
He goes so far I am tired
And at midday I want to sleep.
I want to take a rest.
When the sun is almost down
I return to my house.
There is no food.

THE BOW AND ARROW SONG:
(Sung by the arrow to the bow)

I am alone.
If we were married
We would go out early—
We would kill a deer.

Then it crept in, what I had been waiting for. He began to talk about the gods.

"In the middle of the night, God's hat comes down, and in its shadow the earth becomes dark. It is all striped and spotted (with stars). He Who Rules Earth And Sky is a very ugly-looking god. His clothes are very ugly, more ragged than a poor Seri. He is very dark. His wife is very white.

"The second night *she* comes down, and after three days she goes back to her man. After eight days God comes down. When God came out of the sky he painted the earth different colors, with flowers and trees and grass. They grew up, and the Seris gave them names. The bloodroot is *ah-mehl'*, the mangrove is *kos*, the ocotillo is *hon-has'-sees*, the chamisa is *say'-potl*."

He was off again and Hampton was with him, forgetful of the Seri gods, slowly writing down the words for his vocabulary; but after a while they came back to the subject.

"God comes down to earth and stays eight days, and then he goes back to heaven. He takes with him all the Seris who have died, through a hole in the middle of the sky. For four days the dead Seri lies buried. Then God takes him back through the hole, and there are all the Seris who have died—many, many of them —all *muy contento*, very happy. When they go to heaven they take nothing with them—no bows and arrows, no canoes, no clothes. That is, if they have none on earth. If they are rich here, when they go to heaven they have everything the same up there.

"They hunt and fish just the same as on earth, but they have no troubles and there is always food. There their clothes are pretty—they do not have old rags any more. But their old bodies remain here on earth. Only their bones and blood go to heaven—there is no outside to their body as here. When they get up there, they are never hungry or cold. It is always night up there. After a Seri dies there is no more day for him, but they can see just as well in the dark.

"Only the good people go to heaven. The bad ones stay where they are buried. In the night the dead bad Seris raise their heads out of their graves and look around, but they cannot rise above their shoulders and, before daylight, they sink back. It makes no difference how the moon is, they can see in the dark.

"When the bad ones look out and see the live people, they cry out to them *Wheeeee*, but the live people cannot hear them. When they listen, this sound is very distant and sad, and all the Seris are fearful. When a Seri is traveling alone and hears this call he runs, and the others never go near there.

"When the dead stick their heads out and call, they have no flesh on their faces. Their teeth and bones show very much and they are very frightful. When a man hears this noise he throws off his clothes and runs —and he never goes back for those clothes.

"When a person is buried they do not know whether he is good or bad. They bury with the dead all their goods—their clothes, their bows and arrows; their quivers and any ollas they have—and in a very small pot, made especially, they put food. In another, smaller still, they put water; and, with it, a small shell. The dead one, when he is thirsty, dips up water and takes a little drink. His sandals and knife are placed on his breast, and his face is painted white. Because that is a sign that God has given them, which they must have before they can go through the hole to heaven.

"Four days before a man is to be married he paints his face. An old man getting married does not do this —it is only for his first marriage. A rich man can be married within a year of when he is engaged, but sometimes a poor man who brings only a little water, a little meat, a little food, has to wait as long as three and even four years. During all this time he is serving the girl's mother and family. After a long time passes and he is not diligent in bringing food and water, the mother may send him away and he cannot marry her daughter. If he is once sent away he can then marry only a widow.

"No matter how much food and water he brings, the boy has to spend a year in the house of the mother.

During this year he sleeps outside the mother's house, but cannot have the girl. A little house is built outside the mother's and there the boy sleeps till married.

"About two days before the marriage, the father and brothers build a little brush house for them. It is made beautiful by putting flowers all around inside. For four nights the wedding feast goes on, during which they drink the wine which they make from the cactus-fruit. They don't drink much—not so much that they will fall down. Everybody smokes the wild tobacco, called tobacco-of-the-coyote, in their little clay pipes.

"They are married only when the fruit of the giant cactus is ripe, in May or June. The *pitahaya* fruit is mashed up and put in an olla with warm water, and stirred with a stick for two days. By that time it is fermented and makes them drunk. They also have the *pitahaya* festival at this time, four days, in which they eat the fruit but drink no wine. Two days afterward they brew the liquor and in four days they drink it, with singing and dancing.

"An eight-day feast is held when a child is born. During this fiesta the woman can eat no animal food, with the exception of honey from bees, but she can eat any kind of vegetable foods. Within eight days to six months after the baby is born the mother gives it a name. The mother just gives it a baby name: 'Won't Suck,' or 'Drinks much at the breast,' and the child carries it through life. At the end of six months they feed the baby *atole* (mush), and at the end of a year they feed it meat.

"During this same *pitahaya* season we celebrate the Feast of the Pelican. Five men go to Pelican Island in the night, one carrying a long pole with a torch on top while the others have long poles for killing them. They creep up on the pelicans, which sleep along the shore in the hot weather; and, lying down in the water, light the torch and hold it up. Then they make a noise, the pelicans wake up and raise their heads, and the four men with long poles break their necks. Sometimes they kill as many as forty in a few minutes, while the pelicans are dazed by the light.

"Right there on the beach they skin the birds, saving the fat for grease. They make a pitch from it, to paint the bottoms of their boats, by cooking it with the gum from a dead giant cactus. For two days they cook this and it becomes a very beautiful black paint, which keeps their boats from leaking.

"The meat of the pelicans is roasted on the coals and eaten, but there is no singing and dancing. The women stretch and dry the skins and, in the old days, they would sew them together in sixes to make a blanket; and they would lay many of them together over the ocotillo frames of their houses, to keep out the wind and rain. For this purpose the hides were left crude, because they turned the rain better, and they lasted a very long time.

"Inside the house they spread raw deerskins, to make their beds on, but they never had any woven blankets. The women did not know how to weave. All they wore was a little apron and, over that, a pelican skin. Only in the past few years have they worn clothes from the waist up. Instead of hats they made a wreath around their heads with the leaves of a pretty plant. Men and women both wore them. The men wore a pelican skirt—made of pieces of three pelican skins—around their waists, and that was all. No sandals, because there was no bull hide then, although they sometimes used sea lion and shark skins.

"The Seri women can make a small olla in one day, a very large one in two. They are made with a coil of mud, wrapped against the direction that the sun moves. The earth from which they are made comes from the foot of the mountain on Tiburon Island, but other earth is brought from other parts of the Island. The bulk of the earth used is red.

"The first operation is mashing the red earth. Then it is dried and passed through a sieve, made from a circular band of wood and their own hair, woven fine. They screen it very fine, they add the other earths to harden it. The red earth is for the body of the olla, the other earths are dark. After they are screened and mixed, the clay is started thick at the bottom and brushed upward with a shell.

"The clay is started in the bottom of a basket, like a flat pancake. It is smoothed on the inside with a shell, and a worm of clay is added to the edge. It is pressed and rubbed upward, and each ring as it is added is made thick by rubbing on the inside with the shell, and pressing with their fingers on the outside. Coil after coil is added until it is finished, when it comes to a mouth about six inches across.

"It is dried one day and then burned on a bed of coals made from dry giant-cactus ribs—tipped to one side a little with the mouth up, and another fire around it.

"The oldest ollas were not painted at all. Later they were decorated with blue on red, and the painting was called Feathers of a Pelican. When first burned the pots are very red. To make the paint very blue, they mix a clay with a weed, pounded up in water. They paint it on with the chewed point of a stick. The new olla is kept a long time in the house; after it is old they use it for cooking meat.

"Big, wide-mouthed ollas were used to store water in the desert, buried in the ground and covered with thorny bushes so the coyotes and dogs would not drink from them. They were hidden so nobody could find them, so the Seris always had water."

Several years ago several Seris were called to Guaymas by the padres, who paid each of them three dollars in gold for their Indian names and three pesos for their common names. Santo Blanco was there and the padre paid him eighty pesos to sing and dance these four songs; Dance of the Seris, the Coyote, the Sea Turtle and the Deer. The money nearly filled his hat and the padre told him if he told them to anybody else for less money he would die.

CHAPTER IX

The Holy Cave

SANTO BLANCO had boasted the power to read men's minds, and it was evident he had read mine. He knew that I wanted these particular songs so, apropos of nothing, he brought in the Fathers who had lived at Guaymas and had almost filled his hat with money. They had written the songs down and given him eighty pesos for them.

I remembered the exast words of Corona; "All he thinks about is money!" and observed to Americano that Santo Blanco was getting tired. Then I gave him his peso and told Angelito to feed him well—and in the morning he was back. Back for his breakfast and to tell the Yoris about God and the lesser deities who lived on his Olympus—the high peak of Tiburon. If the Fathers at Guaymas had written down the songs they were safely filed away in the Library of the Vatican, probably to be exhumed a hundred years hence by some research scholar who would say: "Who were these Seri Indians?"

But if I, who was writing down these songs for pleasure and to keep them from being lost, began filling Santo Blanco's hat with pesos I would thereby defeat my own purpose. The price would go up overnight and I would never get the songs. Also I had my doubts about the good Fathers telling him anything about this curse which he claimed hung over him. So I asked him about the Holy Cave which the Indians said lay to the north, and he settled down to talk for the day.

93

"With three other medicine men I went to the Sacred Cave of the Big Mountain. For four days before we visited it, and for the four days we were there, we ate no food and drank no water. When we got inside it was all dark, and all the time we were there it was like night. We lay down together where it was smooth and slept for four days and four nights, after which the Spirit which lives there came to see us.

"He lives in a little cave inside the big cave. I could see through him when he walked toward us, yet I was conscious he was coming closer and closer, until he was a hand's length from my face. It was dark as night, but I could see him. His arms were stretched out and his hands were hanging down, and from their tips water dripped. It was like ice. He came to me very slowly, and held his fingers over my head. He came again and spread his hands over me, and from the finger-tips I caught water in my palms.

"This water is very strong medicine. I give it to a sick man or woman and in three days they are well. If you make this trip to the Holy Cave you never get old like other men. I have none of the holy water now, but if anyone gets sick I can go and get some. Sometimes the color of the water changes.

> From his first finger the water comes clear.
> From his second finger the water comes yellow.
> From his third finger the water comes red.
> From his fourth finger the water comes blue.

"When I go there for holy water the Spirit comes out of his inner cave and sings. This Spirit is a god, but not like the God of the Gringos. He is very much more beautiful than He Who Rules Heaven And Earth, the God in the sky. He has a white hat and a black coat, very long. To his ankles. Inside this black coat there are all kinds of bright colors.

"Ahnt-ah zu'-mah is a great god who came to us from above. He taught us to wear the crown on ceremonial occasions. In the old days the medicine men wore this corona all the time, and especially at dances. He was a little man, so high—about four feet. A white man, with very yellow hair. All his clothes were white, but his sandals were yellow. They were made entirely of deerskin, with the hair on, and fastened with overlapping cords. He came down from the sky to the Seris. They knew him and he knew them. What he knew he learned from the gods.

"When he first came he sat down between two houses and told them to go out and hunt a sea turtle. 'It will be very fat,' he said. Before they went out he drew a picture on the ground of the turtle and he did not move out of his place, east, west, north or south, but sometimes he would go straight down into the earth.

"The next morning the Seris went out and found the *cahuama*. He was so fat his liver was white, and he was full of yellow eggs. Ahnt-ah zu'-mah disappeared into the earth. Before he went he told them to place a tall pole where he sat and on the pole to place a piece of the liver of the fat turtle, and a piece of the fat, and the heart. The next night when he came back he ate all three, and then sat down on the ground.

"The Seris were very happy when they found how fat this turtle was, and they spoke a long speech of thanks for bringing them such a fat *cahuama*. He was with them about a month. Each night he came down from the sky, coming straight down to this spot between the two houses. When daylight came he would disappear into a hole in the earth beneath him. We have never seen him since.

"Ahnt-ah zu'-mah had white clothes all over. He was not the same kind of being as the Spirit in the Cave of God. This Spirit has always been there, and is there yet.

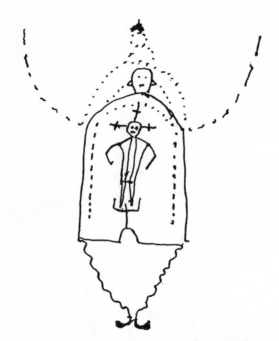

Copy of a picture in the Holy Cave on Tiburon.

In the center is the good god, I Am Very Wise, surrounded by 32 dots for the months he will live on earth. The three crosses from his head indicate that he will never die.

Above him is the bad god, After Four Days The Seris Will Die. He is a mortal, as is indicated by his having ears, and calls the Seris to their death.

Drawing by Santo Blanco.

"The pictures of the Sky and Earth are not in this Cave of God, but in another one on Tiburon Island. The paintings are in colors. The Sky is all in blue except the four roots, which are red. The Earth is all painted white, but the cross in the middle is yellow. There is no black in the pictures. They are painted on a dark wall, but the door of the Cave is white, like ice.

"Another god whose picture is in the cave is I Am Very Wise. His picture is in four colors—blue, red, yellow and white—and the three crosses which extend from his head are the sign of his heart and indicate that he will never die. All Seri gods have this sign. He

A bad god who kills men with his long claws.
Drawing by Santo Blanco.

lives thirty-two months, the number of the dots that encircle him, and then returns to heaven.

"In the same picture, but above I Am Very Wise, is the bad god, After Four Days the Seris Will Die. He is a man, as indicated by his ears—a bad man, who lives only a short time. The gods keep count of his years, and in a very short time they call for this bad god to die. But for good people, the gods count many years before they die. If a man gets very old, this bad god makes him blind. That is just the same as being dead, because he cannot fish or hunt.

"The spots surrounding the bad god in the pictures were placed there by the good god inside—to keep him confined there in the cave. The pedestal at the feet of the good god is placed there for him to stand on, so he will not fall. If he does fall off, he flies all around the mountain, making a noise—*whooo*—like an aeroplane. The wavy lines, supporting the base of the pedestal, represent the walls of the cave. The two curved lines at the bottom are the entrance. This cave on Tiburon is the only one that contains paintings. There is another on the Island having a narrow mouth but wide inside, but the walls are just red rock.

"The *Dioses* or gods who made man are many. The old men have gods and the young men have gods and the children have gods. The gods of the old men come with the longest day of the year and the gods of the young men come only in winter, when the days are shortest. The young men never take any offerings to their gods—only the old men. They take cactus-pears —*pitahayas, sahuaros, sahuertos.* They leave them for the gods, and by the middle of the day they have eaten them. They take three of the big white shells, called *Skey-p,* as big around as the circle of a man's

arms, and lay them at the edge of the water. Then
they put a little water in each one. Then they put in
the *pitahayas,* the *sahuaros* and the *sahuertos* until the
shell is half full. By the middle of the day the gods
have eaten them. And he goes down—the Sun. But
the young men do not bring anything."

CHAPTER X

The Gods and Their Sacrifices

OUR medicine man fell silent in the midst of his disquisition and, looking out, we saw Buro Alazan passing by. I gave Santo Blanco his peso and, when he was starting for home, I slipped him half a peso more. The time had come to raise his pay, for old Sorrel Deer had a sinister look and we could see that Santo Blanco was afraid. These stories he was telling were the property of the tribe, and they might object to our writing them down; but in the morning he came back and continued his stories of the gods.

Ahnt Kai' [he began] is the goddess of the women and children. Ahnt ahs Pok', her little daughter, is the goddess of the girls. Besides these Mahm-m is the special goddess of the women. They add the word mahm-m, which means woman, to that of I Am Very Wise, but speak of her simply as Mahm-m. Another goddess of the young girls is A Daughter of the Gods. She is the daughter of First Woman, and her father is the Sun.

First Woman is also called Painted Woman. Her face and body are painted entirely in blue, but this has no symbolism. It is put on just to look pretty and she is called The Woman Who Is Beautiful. She is a good woman—*pura buena.*

The food of the gods is always vegetable, never animal, and only the fruit of the giant cacti is used as offerings—never seed or *atole.* The women put out

100

small shells in which they have gathered dew, which is a very sweet water. It does not come from the heavens like rain, but it comes out of the sky, about

Ahnt Kai'—Goddess of women and children whose house is on the highest peak of Tiburon, floating in the air. Her little daughter, Ahnt ahs pok', is the goddess of Seri girls, who offer her sacrifices of dew, in white shells.

Ahnt Kai' is the daughter of First Woman by the Sun and corresponds with the Pallas Athene of the Greeks, Kwan Yin of the Buddhists, and the Turquoise Woman of the Navajos. She is represented with wings, with which she flies around at night. The four crosses show that she is holy and at the top are the Sun and the Moon.

Drawing by Santo Blanco.

halfway up, where there are no clouds. This dew is also good medicine. The women and girls do not offer fruit to their goddesses—only dew.

The little boys pray to Ahnt Kai'. The baby boys put out the fruit of the *pitahaya*. The larger ones put out dew-water the same as the girls, only the boys put little flowers in it.

To those who make sacrifices to the gods the god comes down and tells them that they will not die for four years. This is on account of the sacrifices. The gods told the Seris they should not eat their food raw —it should be well cooked. Those who eat raw food will die before those who eat cooked food.

None of the ordinary Seris pray or ask anything directly of the gods. They do not know how to speak to God. The old white-haired medicine man on Tiburon knows, and he taught me. I can speak to the gods. I speak aloud, with my mouth. The gods understand the Seri language. When we talk to the gods we put our hands together before us (like white people) and spread them to the sides as we talk. We do not kneel —we stand upright. When Seris talk to each other they sit down. But when they talk to God they stand up.

There are no bad gods, but the good gods know when men do bad things and punish them.

The Seris have both men and women who can work charms against people. They take the roots of a little plant which grows on the sand dunes and cook it. The red juice which they get from cooking this root, they throw into the eyes of the person they wish to harm, and it makes him sick. *Kwee home-mee'-pay*—"Your eyes need medicine," is the bad word they use when they throw this red water. It is put in their eyes at night, when they are asleep. Gambling medicine is made of the same roots—to make men lose.

Ah kay hai' say kway-ee'-pay are the words they speak. They mean: "This is the medicine of God!" Any god of the old Seris. They take this same root, boil it in water for four days and hang it up to drip through a cloth. It comes out red. Then they put it in the sun for four days and it turns black. Then they let it settle for four days and pour off the water, which is then yellow.

Five different roots are used to make women love men. One is this little seed-plant used in the witch medicine. The others are the roots of the *cholla* cactus, ironwood, mesquite, and the thick stick-cactus. They cook all five roots separately, in much water—then put them in a cloth and let it drip. Mesquite root is yellow, ironwood black, the seed-plant and stick-cactus are red, *cholla* cactus is bluish.

When these are cooked and dripped the juice is caught in four little pots, each of which is tended by a man. When it stops dripping, each man covers the pot with his hand and they carry them all four together and mix them, putting two red ones in first.

This medicine is put in the woman's eyes when she is asleep and it makes her mouth water. After that— she consenting—she wraps her head in a cloth, only her nose and eyes uncovered. Then he asks her if she can see him. If the medicine works she says: "Yes, but I also see the monte and the mountains and the sea and all other things." If it does not work she says: "I can see nothing."

"The Seris make a smoke of swamp-willow inside the house at night, for medicine, and there is another smoke-medicine which only I know. I make a smoke in a cave with palo verde wood and burn a whole tree at night, until nothing is left. When the smoke blows out, the old men, young men, women and children all see it and it makes them go to sleep. This is when I want them all to be asleep.

"The next day all the women of every house come to the cave and get a little bag of ashes, which they guard very carefully. When they get back to their houses, a very little of it is sprinkled over the roof, so no sickness may come. They pay me either with a blanket or two whole white buckskins; or if not that, with a bow and arrows, or a quiver.

"With all this medicine I am not afraid of my enemies. It costs a great deal for medicine, and when the people are poor I do not make any. No, I would not give it to them unless they paid me!"

For some time it had been apparent that Santo Blanco was ill at ease—and he had switched from his stories of the gods to boastful references to his ability as a medicine man. He spoke of witchcraft and charms, of love philters and smoke-medicine. Now he halted in the middle of a sentence and, outside the tent, we discovered Juan Tomas'. The jealous old war chief had crept up and was listening through the canvas. There was a look in his eye like that of a ferret as he peered in through the entrance; and, by the same token, Santo Blanco looked like a rabbit. He was badly scared and, when I handed him his peso, he slipped out the door and was gone.

Americano could do nothing, and very soon he too was gone. It was two days before he returned to camp, except to get a clean shirt; and when we took a walk up the beach we spied him in the Seri village, showing some strange Americans around. The yacht of Kermit Roosevelt had appeared while we were absent and had anchored out of sight behind Pelican Island; and these were some of his guests, who had come ashore and were taking pictures of the Indians. Late that evening, we received a hurried note from Hampton saying that he had gone aboard for the night. The following morning he returned in great haste and rushed off again, to assist in distributing some presents which the party had sent ashore for the Seris.

This is a more or less accepted custom among the pleasure-seekers who visit Tiburon, and it rouses the Indians' savagery to the utmost, having more than once resulted in killings. The Seris' mode of procedure is always the same—first a bold and brazen beggary, a scramble among themselves for the gifts that are handed out; and then, in a flash, they are aboard the boat and snatching at everything in sight. At the first sign of resistance a fight may spring up and—on the Island—the visitors may be killed.

But this was on the mainland, with several sturdy fishermen near to protect the Americans—and Hampton stopped the rush of Indians in time. First he handed out gifts to Chico Romero and the two old war chiefs, who were right up in front with their hands out; and it was not until he opened a carton of cigarettes that the real scramble began. He was passing out the packs, one apiece all around, when Santo Blanco—who had received his share already—came back with his whole family to get more.

Being refused, he reached into the launch—and the trouble began! Hampton struck his hand away; and, while they were quarreling, the rest of the tribe swarmed in, nearly upsetting the boat. Americano leaped out, gave the launch a quick shove, and barely avoided being swamped. It was a dangerous experience for the yachtsmen, who had had a narrow escape from serious injury; and so grateful were they to Hampton, that they kept him aboard a second night.

Meanwhile our researches had been brought to a complete standstill and, when Hampton finally did return, he was so enraged at Santo Blanco that he nearly drove him out of camp. It was very unfortunate that, out of the whole village of Seris, he had happened to have his quarrel with the one particular man we needed most. Santo Blanco must have been in the wrong, from the meek way he took his first cursing; but when, back in the big tent, Hampton began all over again, I intervened. One reproof was enough— we had lost two days already—and Santo Blanco's eyes were beginning to blaze.

The way the sea bass were running, he could earn three times as much with his boat as he was getting for telling stories; and, at any moment now, he might quit. So I suggested to Americano that Santo Blanco was in the position of a guest with us and I thought he had been scolded enough. He was also the chief medicine man of the tribe, without whose help our mission would fail. It took some time to make Hampton see reason and by then Santo Blanco would not talk. But there is one story that it is the delight of every medicine man to tell and I asked him for the story of the Creation. It takes a Navajo four nights to recite the Lasting-From-Long-Ago Chant and when I inquired of Santo Blanco if the Seri people had come up from the underworld through a cane-stalk, he forgot his grievance. But, being miffed, he began with the emergence, and made it brief.

CHAPTER XI

The Creation—and the Seri Gods

IN THE beginning, [said Santa Blanco,] there was a
big *carrizo*, or bamboo, standing out of the earth
and at every joint there were different kinds of people.
At the top were the Seris. Next were the Gringos
(Americans), the Chinese, the Apaches and the
Yaquis. Lowest of all were the Mexicans. Away off by
itself was another joint of cane and in that were the
Papagos, the hereditary enemies of the Seris.

They looked out through knotholes in the cane and
saw a big smoke from God. The Gringo went out first
to meet him, then the Mexican. All the others went
out except the Seris. The Seri wouldn't go out to see
God. When these people went they took presents with
them, all except the Seri, who was too proud. Then
God made them all rich, except the Seri. The Mexicans
he made richest—money, guns, houses, clothes, and
much food. But to the Seri he gave nothing. The
Papago went out but he got nothing for his present—
nothing but his sandals and breechclout. That is the
way they have been ever since. The Seris were poorest
of all—they got nothing. Nothing but seaweed to
cover themselves with, which they had to pull out of
the sea themselves.

The Papagos made their breechclout out of grass.
They took the fiber out of the grass and wove it together with sticks. They had no needles to sew with,
so they used a sharp stick. They took the hide of a wild
pig (*javelina*) and made sandals from it. The sandal

107

strings they made from the skin of a jack rabbit. This was cut in wide strips, because narrow strips would break, and they left the hair on.

The first Seri was a woman called First Woman, or Painted Woman. Her face and body were painted blue, to make her look pretty, and she was spoken of as "The Woman Who Is Beautiful."

She went out of the cane and walked across Tiburon Island to a place where she found a man. They were married and at the end of a year they had a boy. A year later a girl was born. When they grew up they were married and had children. Even though they were brother and sister, they married.

First Man and First Woman had one child, a boy. Then First Woman gave birth to another child—a girl, whose father was the Sun. The woman made a place to lie down by digging a trench in the sand, and the Sun came to her in his own person—not as a man —and she was made with child. That is how the Sun came to this woman—she was lying in a trench in the Sun's rays. The name of the Seri tribe, Kong Ka'-ahk ay mos'-aht, means Children Born of a High Rank Woman. There were six generations where a brother married a sister, and only two children were born of each marriage.

In the seventh generation a woman was born first and her daughter did not marry her brother. She had no brother, so she married the son of one of the earlier generations. The families had all scattered and did not live together. By her husband she had twelve children, all girls, and from these twelve girls came all the Seri families.

The families of these twelve sisters stayed together, and that was the beginning of the Seri Tribe. Kong

Ka'-ahk ay mos'-aht is the name they gave themselves when they all came together.

Ahnt Kai' is the name of the woman whose father was the Sun and she corresponds to Kwan Yin, the Buddhist Goddess of Mercy, and to Est-san ad'-lehi, the Turquoise Goddess of the Navajos. She lives in heaven with the other gods, but she comes down to Red Mountain northwest of here. She taught the women to dance and sing. They dance eight days for the Fiesta of Ahnt Kai'. It is in the hot months, when the cactus-pears are ripe. At that time they gather twenty or thirty baskets of *pitahayas*, and with half of them they make wine. They also gather many baskets of mesquite beans and grind up the pod for mush. Young men and young women and children drink this *atole*. The older men and women drink *pitahaya* wine.

They sing to the *venado* deer and the buro deer and also to the Fish God. In the Fish Dance—in which an old man leads the dancing and singing and a circle of young girls dances with him, singing the same song after him—no married woman can take part. They always hold their skirts out in front of them when they dance the Fish Dance.

There is a Big Chief—Capitan of the Fish—but even he cannot order when a Fish Dance shall be given. Sometimes a whole year passes by without the dance. Only Ahnt Kai' of all the gods can tell when to dance it.

Ahnt Kai' is the special goddess of the women and children. She has no husband but she has a child, a girl, who lives under the ground, by herself. The house where she lives is all shiny and white outside, and painted blue inside. Ahnt Kai''s house is on the highest peak of Tiburon Mountain, but it does not rest

on the mountain. Four roots hold it down, and through
these roots water flows down into the mountain, and
underground until it comes to Arroyo Carrizal. There
it flows out in a little stream, where the buro deer
comes down to drink. In the night the buro comes to
this stream and eats much green grass and drinks.
When daylight is coming he goes up into the high
mountains.

Ahnt Kai' has a bell, like the big church bells in
Hermosillo. It is hidden in the middle of the Island
fifteen leagues from the fresh water at the north end
of the Island. It rings at sunrise, midday and sunset.
She goes to sleep after the third bell, but wakes up at
midnight and rings it again. All the Seris sing about
it, but only Santo Blanco can hear it.

The men do not sing to Ahnt Kai'—only the women.
She has no husband and no relations with men. Her
daughter is just like her but very small—two feet
high. The children sing the *pitahaya* song—no other
—to her. She made the *pitahaya* and gave it to the
children: Ahnt ahs pok' is her name. She is the goddess to whom the children make their offering of dew.
Dew is called fragrant water. In the days long ago,
Ahnt Kai' brought *pitahayas* to her little daughter in
the white house. The little girl found they were so
good that she gave some to the Seri children, and the
Seri children found they were so good that they gave
them to the men to eat. And the men found they were
so good that they gave them to the gods, as sacrifices.

I Am Very Wise is the god to whom the men make
their offerings, in the great shells on the shore. He
lives in the cave on Tiburon. The young boys also
make their offerings to him.

Ahnt Kai' is the goddess who cures snake bites. She

lives in a cave on Red Mountain and in the winter all
the snakes live there, too. They crawl in through a
small hole. When the earth turned over, the Red
Mountain west of here did not, because that is where
she lives. When the hot summer comes the snakes
crawl out of the cave and spread all over the country.
When the cold weather comes they all return.

The rattlesnake originally was not poisonous. But
he got the thorns from an ironwood tree and put them
in his mouth. Now when he bites a Seri the man will
die, unless Ahnt Kai' intervenes by looking at him. In
the middle of the night, when the man who has been
bitten by a rattlesnake is asleep, she comes with a tiny
rattlesnake in her hand and rubs it over the sick man's
chest. If she comes and does that, he is cured. That is
the only cure the Ancients had. Now the Seris go to
Hermosillo and get an injection of black stuff [anti-
venom].

The rattlesnakes have a chief named Big Snake. He
lives on Tiburon Island. He is an enormous rattlesnake and inhabits a cave near the top of the big mountain. There used to be a big water-hole in this cave, but
the Chief Snake swallowed a buro deer and then drank
up all the water in the pool. He is longer than from
here to the Big House [one hundred and fifty yards]
and he is fatter than this tent [twelve feet]. [Prob-
ably a black water-boa.]

When he is hungry he goes out into the brush,
dragging in to him with his tail all the animals in that
circle. Sometimes he eats eight to twelve buros at one
time.

He makes a terrible roar when he is hunting and
you can hear him six leagues away. *Hrrrrrr*—a high,
tremulous note. When he makes that noise it is because

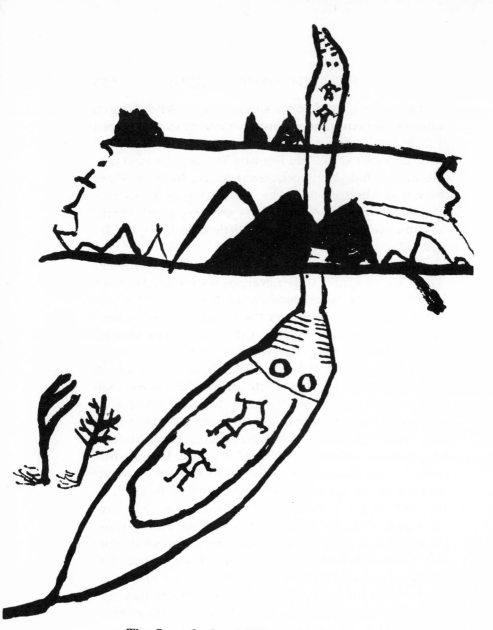

The Great Snake of Tiburon Island.

He ate two men, which made him sick. After darting through a ridge into the sea, he died.

Drawing by Santo Blanco.

he has eaten a lot of buros and is happy. When he gets hungry he comes out of his cave and goes to the west side of the big mountain. When he comes to the valley he crushes down all the trees in his way, he is so big. No matter how big the ironwoods are, he turns them over with their roots in the air. Last year I saw this big snake himself. All the Seris are very much afraid of him. He has no fangs—the little ones have, but he has not.

The Seris never offer sacrifices to the Big Snake. They are so afraid they never go near him. He is so big that if you were standing on the shore here you could see him crawling over the top of Tiburon Mountain [twenty miles away]. A Seri man and woman were walking along, the woman ahead, when they saw a huge thing, red and black, beside the trail. It was the Big Snake and he ate them. But he was not used to eating people, only buro deer and other animals, so it made him sick. He threshed around knocking down big ironwoods and *sahuaros*. With his tail he pulled up a big *sahuaro* and threw it far off, because he was full of pain. He went so fast that when his head struck the mountain he went right through it and into the ocean down into deep water where he lay for a year, sick. At the end he died, from eating people instead of his regular food. The gods made him die. Then the waves floated him ashore, about the middle of the Island, and they found the bones of the two Seris in his belly. The gods told them to pick up his bones and put them in a fire-hole until they were cooked. When this was cold, if they ate of it, no snake could hurt them.

At this time the people spoke all kinds of different languages, and they couldn't understand each other.

One man went without food and water for eight days and, when all these strange people came to see the bones of the snake that had been washed ashore, he came out in the middle of the night and he could speak to any of them. They could understand him and he them. Then all the Seris learned to talk like him, and now they all speak the same language.

The colors of the world came from this pit when they cooked the Big Snake. When they took the bones out there was nothing but soup left. This divided itself into four colors: red, black, blue and white. The man who had fasted eight days spoke to the olla and the olla told him the language through which he talked to everybody else.

There is a Big Pot, as big around as this tent, that was in this hole. The gods pulled it out and moved it up on the mountain. The Seris are afraid to go there, because some of them had heard this olla speaking in a strange language. The outside of the Pot is decorated with a row of figures like white dolls. It is about the span of a man's hand thick, and the mouth is very wide—not like a Seri olla. When you are far from this cave at night you can see it, because it shines like a lantern. In the daytime many people have seen smoke, very black, coming out of this olla. At sunset the smoke, even if it reaches up to the clouds, dies down; and when it gets dark you can see this light, like a lantern.

Ahnt Kai' told the Seris years ago that when they killed a rattlesnake they were to burn him. The Big Snake does not care if they kill the ordinary rattlesnakes, so they kill them. Sometimes they catch a rattlesnake and sew up his mouth and turn him loose on the desert. It makes no difference if he cannot eat.

He will not die. They just sew up his mouth so he can't bite them. Sometimes after two years they find one of these snakes with its mouth sewed up and he has grown much larger. They try him with their foot to see if he can bite. If he can't, they cover his head with green leaves and let him go, because Ahnt Kai' told them to do that.

On top of the big mountain on Tiburon there are two nests of enormous size. One is of the Eagle, who is so big that he can carry off a full-grown deer. The mother bird lays eggs as big around as the circle of a man's arms, and the nest has been there since the first Seris came to the mountain. They still live there. Their eggs are pink, with brown spots scattered far apart. There are four skulls of Seris, without hair or other bones, at one end of the nest. The other nest is not so big, but around it are scattered great piles of fish bones. It belongs to the mother of the Pelican which lived there for many years.

If a Seri breaks one of the eagle's eggs she will come down and seize him by the head and carry him off. But if he just hits the egg and does not break it the eagle will not hurt him. The male eagle kills only male buro deer and the female eagle kills only female.

The Seris are not afraid of the Pelican. Because it has no teeth it cannot tear their skins. The children are afraid of the big raven. If a child breaks a raven's egg, the raven who is up in the sky, will come down and pluck out one eye. There is also a bird like a duck, but with a beak like sharp knives. If a Seri tries to take away eggs from him the sharp knives will cut his hands very badly. This is the Frigate Bird. His nest is on the Island, and on a little island near here.

CHAPTER XII

Man Who Built Fires

FROM the way Santo Blanco had taken his reproof that morning and then gone right ahead with his stories it was evident he was of a long-suffering and forgiving disposition—either that, or he needed the money. John Hampton, after speaking his mind, retired into a frigid silence which had become almost a habit of late. After associating with a son of Theodore Roosevelt and the guests on his yacht, it was quite a change to interpret for a boat-robbing Seri. But he treated him so considerately that the next morning our White Saint returned.

Santo Blanco was hardly a saint, as his name implies, but he set us an example in forbearance by telling one of his very best stories. It was about Ahnt ah koh'-mah—He Who Built Fires—who taught his people how to live. He is the Hiawatha of the Seris— the Wise Man who came among them so long ago that they did not know how to make a fire.

Many years ago, Santo Blanco said, a white man, tall with a white beard, came over the water from the west, in a boat that moved by itself, without paddles. All the Seris on the Island saw him coming. He was dressed in the skins of pelicans, deerskins and rabbit skins, all white. He came to Patos Island, the little island to the north, and from there the Seris invited him to Tiburon. He landed at Tecomate and went all around the Island, and at each point he taught them different things to eat.

At each camp, on each point of land, he would

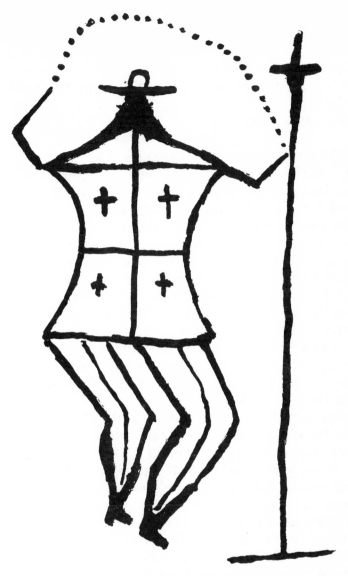

Ahnt ah Koh'-mah—He Who Builds Fires. A tall, bearded man with long hair, who taught the Seris how to live. He carries a cross, which bores into the earth. The dots are the 27 houses of the ancient Seris.

Drawing by Santo Blanco.

show them how to kill some animal that lived there, and they would build a fire and eat it—a different

Santo Blanco's map of Tiburon Island.

At the first point is the turtle, then the buro deer, third the jack rabbit, fourth the wild pig, fifth the fish, sixth the crab, seventh the shark, eighth the sea lion, ninth the porpoise, last the maguey plants.

Ahnt ah Koh'-mah named each point for the food they ate there and he made trails from the beach to the water-holes.

animal at each point. At the first point the turtle, then
the buro deer, the jack rabbit—fourth the wild pig,
fifth the fish, sixth the crab, seventh the shark, eighth
the sea lion, ninth the porpoise. And, at Estevan Island,
the maguey plants.

All around the Island, at each point, he would show
them something else to cook and eat. Before then the
Seris had eaten their food raw, because they had no
fire. He showed them how to use smoke for signals.
When the people saw his big smoke they would go to
him. Also he taught them that, when they saw the
smoke going into the sky, they could go there and get
fire and bring it.

He named each point after the food they ate there.
Before then they had eaten the seeds of the mangrove
trees, green or dried; of the grass, and of a little weed
like pigweed. Before he came, the Seris ate only vegetable food. They did not know how to eat cooked meat.
Ahnt ah koh'-mah did not teach them to wear clothes.
That they knew already. One of the old men had
learned how to make buckskin and to soften hides.
Now almost everyone knows.

He taught them to live in houses and showed them
how to build one on each point. He also taught them
to live together, as man and wife, in these houses. On
the three points at the south end of the Island they
did not build any houses, but he taught them to go
there—and on the first point they would catch sharks,
on the next porpoise, and on the last sea lions. He
took them to San Estevan Island where the agave
grew, and taught them to roast the mezcal head, but
he did not teach them to make mezcal liquor.

Ahnt ah koh'-mah opened trails into valleys in the
mountains where there was water. Each three points

had trails going to the same water. There were six places where they could get water after rain. But, except when it rained, there was no water on the west side of the Island. Then there were tanks.

He taught them to make little-mouthed ollas and to hide them underground. They were buried and covered up, so the coyotes and dogs could not drink from them. Each olla was big enough to hold water for a whole family for three or four days. He taught the women to make these ollas thin, and the men to make bows and arrows.

He taught the people on the Island not to quarrel and have *barullos* among themselves. There was always trouble on the mainland, at Tepopa and Tastiota, but on the Island there was peace. Everybody on the Island was very happy—until a man came from the mainland and stole a girl and took her away. This was five hundred years ago. Ahnt ah koh'-mah went with the people of the Island to fight the family of this man. The three brothers of this girl fought the men of that family and killed the man who had stolen her, and his father, and took her back to the Island.

Ahnt ah koh'-mah taught them to spear sharks off the rocks. They speared them in the back of the head with a lance-point made of the hard tap-root of the ironwood, which grows straight down, very long. They ate the flesh of the shark, but not the liver, guts, fins or head. At that time they did not know how to make oil from shark's liver, but they try it out now.

Porpoises were speared with a double-pointed spear, to hold them better. They got them where a rock jutted out over the sea using a rope made of mesquite root. They hold the line in one hand and the spear in the other. Then they drag them ashore and kill them with a rock.

A long time ago the pelicans used to sleep on the

Man on a rock, spearing a shark with two sea turtles in its stomach.

Drawing by Santo Blanco.

rocks and the Seris would sneak up on them with a long pole and give them a wallop, to break their necks. This was in the dark, and they could only get two or three—and only approach them once. Now they go out with a light on a long pole—a dry *pitahaya*-cactus rib. They tie firewood to the end with green swamp-willow strings, and used to kill a lot at one time, but now they are too lazy to hunt them.

They had no balsas then from which to kill sea lions, so they waited till the lobo came ashore and went

Seri spearing a sea lion from the rocks.
Drawing by Santo Blanco.

to sleep. Then, from the rocks, they would spear him in the soft place at the back of the head, with a very heavy ironwood spear. Even that would only stun him, so they dragged him up on the shore and killed him with stones.

They ate only the fins of the sea lion, using the raw hide to make a skirt for the women and the tanned hide to make a skirt for the men. For the women's skirts, they pounded the hide to make it a little soft. The skirts made of buro-hide were very soft and they were used as mantles, to cover themselves in cold weather.

The first skirts worn were of pelican skins. They began by using these, then deer skins; and then all kinds, like sea lion, mountain lion, wild pig, and tiger skins. Then one of the Seri captains got from some people in the east a skirt made of manta-cloth. They called this cloth *es ko toh'n* and made shirts of it which had no sleeves and no neck, but just slipped over their heads and reached just below the armpits or nipples. (This *camisa* is found clear down the Coast, to Tehuantepec and Central America.)

The first one was ready-made and was given them by white people, and the Seris learned to make others from it. The blouses which the women now wear came from the Yaquis. They were made of cotton cloth and were the same shape as the men's shirt. The Seri women learned to make their skirts from the Yaquis. That is why they are so long. All the Yaqui women who came to Tiburon used to wear them that way. The women wear long skirts in winter because they are warm. In summer they wear them anyway, even if they are hot.

The Seri men now wear red handkerchiefs and flour sacks around their waists, just as a custom handed down from old times when they wore nothing else. They had no pantalones then. The first breechclouts were of pelican skin. In the old days they wore no sandals, but used the green leaves of the mesquite to cover their feet. When the shoots first grow out they have no thorns on them. The thongs of the sandals were made from mesquite roots twisted together in loops. A cord passes underneath the ball of the foot and comes out over the instep, where it meets another thong coming up from between the big toe and the second toe.

In the night time, Ahnt ah Koh'-mah opens up— like a paper doll—and becomes double. In the daytime he folds together again and is one man. At night he rides around on the ancient rattlesnake and watches to see if the Seris obey his orders. He lives in the middle of the Island—in the earth, not in a cave—and he is not buried. He can look out and see anybody, on the mainland as well as on the Island. He is a god and he is a man, too. He has lived in the middle of the Island many years, but he never drinks water nor eats food.

He ordered the women not to feed their babies solid food too soon, or they would die. Their food should be cooked. He also told them that, when they are roasting mesquite beanpods, they should put a little earth into the pot. When they can get them they eat the acorns of white oaks. Ahnt ah koh'-mah taught the Seris how to cook them, and all the other food that they eat.

The Papagos knew how to cook preserved cactus-pears, but the Seris did not. Because the Papagos had to go so far to get fruit, they stored it a long distance from their villages, and sometimes the Seris would find it and eat it. In the old times the Seris stored seeds of the *pitahaya*, *sahueso*, eelgrass and ironwood in a cave, because the cave was dry, but they do not do so now. They do not have to any more, because they have guns to shoot game and iron spears to get sea turtles with.

Now they keep food for only one day. Before, they had four or five pots full of seeds stored in caves. They did not eat them in hot weather but kept them for winter. The women still know how to make the big, thin, storage ollas; but they do not make them now because both men and women are working for the fishermen, and in the oysters, and they can buy food at the store. A woman could make a big olla in three days, if she had the material. If the pot is dry at noon they can fire it and have it done by dark.

The Seris at Tastiota and Tepopa were accustomed to store seeds, but those on the Island never stored anything. But sometimes now, if there are lots of ironwood seeds, they gather a little and keep it till it is eaten up.

It doesn't matter much if they have no food for a day or two, if they have a little water. And pretty soon they can kill a rabbit or a deer or get a turtle or fish or crab; and if they are hungry they can eat clams. In the lagoon there is a small clam that they can eat, but they never ate oysters in the old days. They didn't know they were good to eat until the white men came, about ten years ago, and began buying them. Now the Seris like them very much.

CHAPTER XIII

Seri Clans

AFTER First Man and First Woman married and had children, [he went on], for six generations a brother married a sister. Then there was no brother and the girl married the son of another pair who had moved away. Her name was Kee-mee'-kay ahn ko'-ahn, Woman with Many Children—and from her twelve daughters sprang all the Seri Clans.

Kee-mee'-kay is the mother's family name. Each of the daughters carried that name—the rest is just for her. The first daughter was:

> *Kee-mee'-kay ah pay'-ket-ee*—First Girl.
> "   "   "   *ee-quop'*—Second Girl.
> "   "   "   *ee-kee quop' hah*—Third Girl.
> "   "   "   *ee-kee-so'*—Fourth Girl.

"That is all I can remember. If I talk with God tonight I can remember the rest."

Tahm was the father of the twelve girls—and the same word is now used for Man. From these four daughters are descended the four Seri Clans, and until lately they lived separate from each other:

The Coyote People lived at Poso Pina in the mountains on the mainland.
The Pitahaya People lived on the flats of the mainland.

The Turtle People lived on the southwest point of the
 Island.
The Pelican People lived on the southeast point of the
 Island.

Years ago brothers and sisters could marry each
other, but not now. Cousins could marry, but not now.
The women on the Island cannot marry Island men,
but mainland men. The Coyote, Pitahaya, Turtle and
Pelican People now can marry within their clan—it is
just that the people of the mainland must marry people
from the Island.

Santo Blanco's wife came from the Island and he
came from Tepoca, on the mainland. His father was
Antonio Noriega and, when Hermosillo was only two
houses, he was the chief of the Tepoca branch.

There are many fishermen at Puerto Libertad—
Yaquis, Yoris, Mexicans. They have tents and brush
houses, but there is always a *barullo* going on and the
Seris never go up there. Manuel Encinas has three
sons and a daughter up there, but he never sees them
any more. The Germans and the Yaquis are fighting
all the time, but the Americans and the Mexicans get
along well together. It is the Germans and the Yaquis
who make trouble for the Seris. Manuel doesn't know
whether his children are dead or alive. The Germans
and the Yaquis kill the Seris. About a month ago, on
New Year's night, a man came down on foot alone
and said there was a big *barullo* going on and he didn't
know whether they were all killed or not.

At Pueblo de Seris, near Hermosillo, there was
formerly a Seri named Kolusio, who had been captured as a boy. The Mexicans made him a schoolteacher and he tried to teach the Seris. He was a good

man and used to come out and visit the Seris, but they didn't learn any Spanish from him. He is dead now. In his time the smallpox came and many, many Seris died. The rest escaped from Hermosillo and ran away out here.

They make medicines out of herbs and some are very good, but they have no way of curing smallpox. All die—the big and the little. The Government sent a man out here eight years ago who vaccinated all the Seris. A little while afterward a man who did not like them gave them some clothes which were infected with smallpox, but none of their people died. The Government saved them with its medicine. Santo Blanco said he knew nothing of sickness or medicine—when God calls people they go.

The Seris have two little wooden gods which they hang up in the sacred caves, tied together with a string, and when people are sick they put them on their breasts. It is the same as the Yoris' medicine. The two-legged god stays eight days in the cave, the one-legged god stays twelve days.

They go to the caves of the gods, but they are not gods. They can be painted in any color—red, blue or black. The hats on their heads show they are men. If they were gods they would have a cross on them. "Anybody can make these figures, but I can carve them best. When someone is sick we put the two-legged figure in some cave in the mountains, the higher up the better, and he is left without food and water for eight days. He gets tired of that and the man will get well, because the god will come out to get food and water.

"The two-legged god can only stand it eight days in

the cave—the one-legged one can go twelve days. They hang up the two-legged god first, in the hope that the sick people will get well quick. If they do not, they put the other one in the cave. As they approach the cave they sing to the figure, and if the person is going to get well the spirit of the little figure will come out.

"Anybody can take the sick person to the cave, and when the sick one gets well they know that the spirit of the figure has come to them. They leave the figure in the cave then. There are several caves, but the high ones are best. For four days they sing songs to these figures, called:—I Am Singing That You May Cure.

"The figurine is held out to the four directions, while the eyes are fixed upon it. Then, at the end of the song, the image is held at arm's length. If it trembles, the medicine is no good. When they sing to the one-legged god and the patient is getting well, the wind begins to blow. If it does not blow he will not get well.

"There is a cave in which the wind blows, called: Cave of The Wind. It is on top of the Big Mountain on the Island. Sometimes we go there to cure people, but the patient is left at home. The only time we sing to the wind is when somebody is sick. If it blows strong, we sing to it. Sometimes, when there is no wind outside, it blows inside—sometimes for four days. The songs are not addressed to the wind, but to the figurine that makes it blow."

The medicine man's pay in the old days was a complete balsa, with ropes and everything. That is a value of fifty pesos. Now they pay Santo Blanco a good canoe, worth as much as two hundred pesos—or so he says. The sick man will never die if he sings over him. He sings over him at midday—and for four nights. Then he can see the insides of the patient and find out what is wrong. He gives them no medicine in the mouth—it is just the singing that cures them.

If a person is going to die, his blood is very black. If he is going to get well, his blood is red. When they are sick, if their head is sick Santo Blanco looks in the head. If their belly is sick he looks in the belly. If their back, he looks there. If they are going to die, the flesh inside is all black and their bowels are yellow. He sings when he looks into the patient. He sings to the sickness. It is a spirit, or a figure, which appears there. This is how a sick man looks when he looks into him. It is as if he had glasses on. He can see what could not otherwise be seen.

The body of a patient as it appears to Santo Blanco, the medicine man, when he looks into it after singing his twelve songs.

Drawing by Santo Blanco.

Santo Blanco charges five pesos for the one-legged god. If you hang one of the figurines with two legs up in your house no sickness will come. They are the House Gods. The one-legged one has two legs at night. If you hang them up, the span of your arms away from each other, all around the house, no sickness will come to you, and they can be used over and over again.

When Santo Blanco sees the sickness, it comes out where he sees it. He sings to the sickness—twelve songs. In all sickness, including smallpox, when he sings twelve times, it will come out. He does not rub the patient or suck the spot. He just looks into them and at the twelfth song the sickness comes out, but if they are going to die he can't make the sickness come out.

CHAPTER XIV

The Quarrel Between the Men and the Women

FOR two days Santo Blanco had talked about the gods and, without the least fear, described the religion of his people. But I noticed that he did not sing. He gave in the greatest detail the history of the Seris; and his account of the coming of Ahnt ah koh'-mah revealed him a true culture hero, like the Star Child of the Northern Indians. While he had been singing his brief medicine songs Buro Alazan had appeared and looked in at him, but even then Santo Blanco paid no attention.

On the third morning, however, it was evident they had had trouble; for Santo Blanco warned me to wrap up the figurines I had bought, or there would be more bad winds and storms. But, after I had done that, he still sat in gloomy silence, and I saw I would get no more songs that day. Still, whatever he told was valuable and, in order to get him started, I inquired if the Seris, like the Navajos, had ever had a quarrel between the men and the women. He admitted, though reluctantly, that such had been the case; and finally blurted out that, except for one thing, a similar quarrel might start, any time. The women had not got angry enough to drive the men away—that was all.

Since he would not proceed I told him the Navajo story, which is as follows:

A long time ago the Navajos lived by a wide stream which flowed both ways at once; and the wife of the

chief, by being unfaithful to her husband, started a
quarrel which separated the people. All the men took
the part of the chief, and all the women that of the
wife. They began arguing about which could get
along best without the other, the men or the women;
and it ended in the men crossing the stream that ran
both ways, leaving everything they had for the women.

The first year the women had lots of corn and food;
whereas the men, having nothing, had to exist by
hunting. But the second year the women, becoming
despondent, neglected to plant the fields; and at the end
of four years, they were ragged and hungry. The
men, however, cleared fields at their new home and
planted them, killed deer and made buckskin clothes,
and built new houses to live in. But they were not
happy and, at the end of the fourth year of their trial,
they returned to the swift-flowing river and the chief
went across, just at dusk, alone. He appeared by his
wife's house and she ran to meet him. Then all the
other men came home—and they have been boss ever
since.

While Hampton was interpreting this story to
Santo Blanco, our old enemy, Juan Tomas', appeared
in the doorway and refused to go away. Buro Alazan
came also, and both listened intently. Then Buro Alazan tried to tell the Seri version of the story but Santo
Blanco shut him up. He had become very angry, and
I made them go away and give him a chance to talk.

It had suddenly come over me that this river which
ran both ways at once might be El Infiernillo, the channel between Tiburon and the mainland. As the tides
and great bores sweep up the Gulf, part of the
water flows directly through the channel, while the
rest, rounding the upper end of the Island, turns

south till the two streams meet, passing each other in great tumult. Here, indeed, is a river which flows both ways at once, though the present-day Navajos have no knowledge of its existence. They think that this peculiar stream lies far to the north, and that one river flows *across* the other. In fact, they have no idea how this could take place, it has been so many years ago.

But here the Navajo story closely paralleled their own and, by questioning Santo Blanco on every point, I finally extracted the Seri version from him. Yes, they had had a quarrel. Yes, it was about a woman. The men had gone away. Yes, they had come back— yes, the chief had crossed the river first—yes, it was just before dark. But, instead of becoming boss, the men had been bested in the quarrel—which had been going on ever since.

It was only part of the long story of a matriarchy which had tried for centuries to rule Seriland, and Santo Blanco finally went back to the beginning and told it as it happened.

"About six generations ago—it may be more because it has been told from one mother to another—a man wanted to have two wives. He was already married, but he wanted this other woman, who was already with child by him, though unmarried. The women of the tribe objected, not because she was a *señorita* and with child, but because he did not have the clothes, or meat, or bows and arrows, to support two families.

"He took this woman, anyway, and all the women joined together and caused a *barullo* and drove all the men off Tiburon. This took place at the north end of the Island at a place called Agua Dulce. The women would not even allow them to take water when they left, and the men crossed to the mainland and went to Poso Pina.

"This man, when married, lived with his new wife only four days. Then the mother of the second wife organized all the women against him, because he had taken her daughter. The mother pulled the girl one way and the man pulled the other, and that started her to crying. Then the first wife's mother fought with the second wife's mother, and that made the first wife cry.

"The man went into the mountains to hunt rabbits and, while he was gone, the mother of the second wife took her off to a cave. When the man came back and found his woman gone, all the men sided with him to get the second wife back.

"This was the first time a man had ever tried to have two wives. The women drove all the men away with clubs. They had nothing when they left the Island —nothing but their hands. The women had taken their weapons away from them. When they landed at Poso Pina, the men made knives out of bones and went far to the north. The reason why they had been disarmed was that the women were very angry and made a big *barullo;* but the men were not angry—so they were driven away. For the four years they were away the women lived alone on the Island and were very happy, because without the men there was no *barullo.*

"During the four years the men followed up the Coast a long way, then turned and went a long way east. Wherever they went they found no towns or people. They went east so far they could see the big mountains [Sierra Madres] then turned south and at last came home again.

"When the men came back, the women were very glad to see them and welcomed them to the Island. Each man went back to his own wife. The man who had wanted to marry the second wife had not gone away with the other men. He had been driven out by the women, but came back to his first wife and did not live with his second wife any more. She stayed by herself there in the village. The men built houses and everybody was very happy.

"When the men came back, one went over first in the only old balsa that was left. It took the men five days to cross. The chief went to see his wife first, and at dusk. She told all the others, and the next day all the women were very happy. The women said if the men would come back there would be no more *barullo*. Then the chief went back and told his men and they returned home.

"This old quarrel was like the one going on now. Nacho Romero, brother of the chief, Chico Romero, wanted to take a second wife, a woman by whom he has had a child. He did not have the goods to warrant it and it had caused a row between him and the girl's father. Nacho had taken this girl out into the brush for eight days, and she had a child by him. But there was this difference—the girl's father and Nacho had not quarreled, and the women had not got angry enough to drive the men away. The woman has been taken away from Nacho, and she and her baby are living by themselves. This woman can never marry anyone else, and she cannot marry Nacho. That is what they are fighting about.

"No, the Seris have never told the story of their

quarrel to the Navajos. They have never heard of them, although they know about the Apaches. They told it to the Yaquis—in the early days when they were friendly—but now they are enemies.

"During the trouble, when the Government tried to deport all the Yaquis, many of them had come to live on the Island to escape the soldiers. But the soldiers and Papagos came across and killed a great many men, women and children. The soldiers also killed many Seris. [This was probably only about thirty-five years ago, when the Mexican Government rounded up all the Yaquis and shipped them to Yucatan from Guaymas. Four ships came up to the Island and took the Yaquis far away, and the Seris never saw them again.]

"The Seris could understand the Yaqui language in the old days, but not now. None of the Seris can understand Yaqui. The ancient language that Juan Tomas' speaks is the same as the Yaquis spoke then. Some of the Yaqui women married Seri men on the Island. In the time when they could speak each other's language they intermarried, but not now. The Yaquis are an old people, but the Seris are older. They used to allow the Yaquis to come here and fish, but one time the Yaquis came to the Island and they had a battle. Four Yaquis were killed and four Seris. Since then they have been enemies, and nobody has been able to talk with the Yaquis.

"When Hermosillo was started the first the Seris knew about it, there was one house built against a hill —and the people who lived there were Yoris, who planted watermelons, beans and corn. All around them was nothing but the monte—wild land. The Seris would go there and gather squashes, corn and beans, and take them out and eat them. They also caught a hen and rooster out in the brush and ate them. The Yoris had cattle and horses, too. More people came there to live. There were lots of cattle; but none of them, old or young, had brands. The Seris did not kill horses or cattle at first; but when they found a dead one, the owner would give it to them to eat."

At this point Buro Alazan came back, ostensibly to bring some grass for Angelito's horse, but really to shut Santo Blanco up. He fell silent and when I pressed him with questions, his answers became very brief.

The only battle that Santo Blanco knows about between the Papagos and the Seris was at Tepoca. The Papagos had stored a big olla full of preserved *pitahaya* fruit in the brush and had kept it there for two years. The Seris found it and stole it and took it to Tepoca. The Papagos got ready for battle, very angry, and a great many of them came down and attacked the Seris. The battle was fought with bows and arrows on both sides and the Seris used their *huffts*, or fighting stones.

The battle lasted six days and the Seris drove the Papagos back to their own country. Many were killed on both sides. It was the use of the stone *huffts* that decided the battle. The Papagos had never seen the stones used before, and only six of them got away. There were more than fifty Seris killed, and more than one hundred and twenty Papagos. Only the Tepoca Seris fought in the battle. None of the others knew of the fight till it was over. They fought both in the night and the day—as did the Papagos also.

This was all that Santo Blanco could remember about the wars of his people while Buro Alazan, the old war chief, was around. So, still trying to compare them with the Navajos, I asked him if the Seris had a story about the Great Gambler of Kintyel, who won so many people that their relatives, to reclaim them from slavery, built the great Pueblo Bonito for him. This hero, He Who Wins People, was a son of the Sun, having blue eyes and yellow hair; and, when the gods got together and broke him, he ascended into the sky and is supposed to have gone south into Mexico, where later he became king of the Mexicans.

It was a far call, but Santo Blanco knew all about him; showing that at some time there had been some connection.

"Tee-el'-lah—Earth, was the Great Gambler. Every grain of sand on earth knows how much he gambled. His father was En-tih' hah-kah—Had Lots of Cows. He lived long ago but after the Mexicans came. He gathered wild cattle in the brush and kept them. His mother was En-een tihk'—Milks the Cows. He had no shirt at first. Then he won a buckskin to put over his shoulders, and a skirt to go around his waist. Then he won the children of the people he gambled with. Then he won two pots full of water and a yoke-stick to carry them. Then he won a house, and the wood to build a fire. He won a hundred houses, until there were no more to win. He was like the Government— he owned everything. Only one man would not gamble with him."

The shadow of Buro Alazan was cast against the white of the tent, and Santo Blanco lost his memory entirely. He did not know why the gods had told the Seris not to eat the desert chipmunks—the little ground-squirrels that undermined the sand dunes and made them impassable for the Mexican cavalry—and

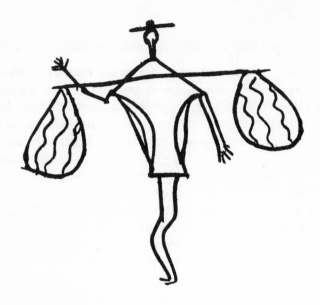

The Great Gambler won two pots full of water and a yoke-stick to carry them home. Then he won even the children of the people he played with until there was nothing left to win. He was like the Government—he owned everything.

Drawing by Santo Blanco.

so on. Then he mentioned once more that the padres
at Guaymas had paid him a great price for telling
them the four songs that I wanted. The first time he
had told me this story the price given had been eighty
pesos, but now it was one hundred and fifty. I could
see that I was about to lose my valued little medicine
man so I reached into my pocket and handed him over
his peso. Then I told him that, since the padres already had the four songs, I no longer wanted them
and he took the hint to depart.

CHAPTER XV

The Big Barullo

WITH Santo Blanco gone and old Buro Alazan hanging around to drive any other aspirants away, it looked as if he had a cinch on the job; but I did not like the way the old war chief had been acting and told him I was tired of writing. What I was really tired of was having him and Juan Tomas' deliberately intimidating my medicine man, and I told Angelito to get another man to bring in grass for his horse. This cut Buro Alazan off from the breakfast he had been receiving and got him out of the way. But by this time, alas, Santo Blanco had gone on a big drunk, along with the rest of the tribe.

It ended in the worst *barullo* ever known at Kino Bay, a brawl so violent and all-inclusive that it left the village a wreck. Santo Blanco, our mild-eyed little mentor, had tried to whip Chico Romero, the young chief—and at last the whole story came out. The mysterious woman that Chico's brother had stolen was Santo Blanco's own daughter, Ramona; and my innocent inquiry concerning a quarrel between the men and the women had thrown him into a villainous mood. After a couple of drinks of fire-water, the memory of his wrongs had overcome him—he had picked out the biggest man in the tribe and tried to work him down to his own size.

This was just a starter for the general fight which had followed and which continued most of the night; and in the morning Juan Tomas' was found almost dead, with two of his ribs kicked in. He had fallen across the entrance of his daughter's house; and the drink-mad carousers, stumbling over his body, had nearly caved in his whole chest. Besides this injury, he had caught a bad cold from lying out in the wind; and at Hampton's request, I contributed some medicine to keep it from turning into pneumonia.

The morning after was a sad affair, with everybody either crawling around in a daze or looking for some-one to continue the fight. We kept out of it entirely, but Americano was everywhere, ministering to the sick and interceding in the quarrels, trying to find out what it was all about. It really went back to this love affair between the Chief's brother and Santo Blanco's daughter, whom Nacho wanted to take as his wife. But he was already married and did not have the goods to support a second wife, even if the elder women would consent to polygamy, against which they had been fighting for years.

For six generations, as Santo Blanco had related, this problem had always been with them; especially as the men, from so many being killed in war, were greatly outnumbered by the women. For the good of the tribe—which time and again had been reduced al-most to extinction—it was necessary that the survivors should take more than one wife. Either that, or let the women find husbands outside the tribe.

But the women had something to say about that, and on both counts they voted an emphatic No. Ac-cording to their system of marrying off their daugh-ters, the prospective sons-in-law had to serve them, virtually as slaves, for from one to two or three years. And, if they failed to prove they were good providers, they were denied the girl of their choice and could then marry only widows. Against this matriarchal tyranny the men were constantly fighting, but even the threat of tribal extinction would not bring the clan mothers to yield.

Santo Blanco's valiant attempt to whip Chico Romero had started the quarrel all over again; and when, on the following day, we visited the Seri village, it was still going on at white heat. In front of the brush shade which sheltered the chiefs and their supporters, four hard-faced women sat in a half-circle, all talking at once. When their chatter died down, some man would make a facetious remark and it would rise to new heights of fury—and all the time, at the door of her well-built house near by, Ramona sat alone. Even her baby had been taken away from her, and was being cared for in Chico's camp. When no one was looking she would slip over and hug and kiss it.

According to their old law, both the mother and the child should die. She was a pretty girl, this Ramona, the only member of the tribe who could read and write. To obtain this education she had lived with a Mexican family for several years; but, while getting it, she had apparently picked up some free-and-easy ideas about morality. She was quite a problem in more ways than one, and enough passion was being expended over her fate to start a small-sized revolution.

Her brush house was built square, in Mexican style; and as she sat, dressed in red cotton, in its doorway, she was nonchalantly smoking cigarettes. She was the first girl in the tribe to step out and adopt the Mexican ways, and the results had not been auspicious. But she was a high-spirited woman and, when drinking, was reputed to have a violent temper—quite a

One of the scolding matriarchy, determined that Nacho should not take Ramona for his plural wife.

(Photograph by Dane Coolidge)

The wild Seri—just over from Tiburon—drunk and demanding
more.   (Photograph by Dane Coolidge)

Seri face painting in blue and white, symbolizing a pelican's wing.
It is the art of women whose only canvas has been their own faces.
                                         (Photograph by Dane Coolidge)

modern problem child for poor Santo Blanco to worry over.

He sat off by himself, very melancholy and chap-fallen, and did not look up when we passed; so the next day, when he did not appear for duty, we engaged the insistent Buro Alazan. He seemed to think he had something to impart without which our researches would be as nothing, and we let him have his way. Perhaps, if he could get it off his chest, he might go away and leave us alone. He was a war chief, second only to Juan Tomas', and the first thing he did was to correct Santo Blanco's story about the battle with the Papagos at Tepoca.

The Papagos, said he, were preparing for a Fiesta and had a big olla filled with *miel*—syrup made from cactus-pears which they had gathered in Seriland— at Tepoca. The Seris knew of this and, when the Papagos hid it and went away, they dug it up and held the feast instead.

When the Papagos found out about it a great number of them came down and drove the Seris off, killing several. The Seris went south and got others, then they went north and had a big battle of one day. They killed many of the Papagos, because they could run faster. They also had better bows and arrows, and at last they charged on what Papagos were left and killed them with stones.

The Seris placed a man and his family at a water-hole, Poso Coyote, and he watched. Every time the Papagos came down into the Seri country he would send his sons to the Island for help, and they would al-ways kill the Papagos. At that time the Seris did not fight at night. They never have fought at night. Their manner of attack was to spy on their enemies until they went to sleep. Then they would creep up on them and, when the people got up at daylight, they would let fly their arrows and kill many of them. They would fight in the day and eat and rest at night.

The Seris never fought with ahsts, or rocks, except when there was a battle and they came to close quarters. In an ordinary fight their bows and arrows were so much better than those of the enemy that they did not have to use stones. They always used surprise attacks when they could.

The Seris had had trouble with the Mexican ranchers, and the ranchers killed many of them. So the Seris prepared to fight them. They carried all their women and children across from the Island to the mainland in balsas and were camped at Poso Pina preparing for battle, when the Mexican soldiers arrived. The Seris were getting ready for a War Dance and were in a circle. They had started circling around, each fully armed, all yelling.

One would sing a War Chant, and then all would yell. Then another would sing and all would yell, but there was no music except that of the boca or mouth. The warriors did not paint their own faces, but when they were getting ready for battle the women would do it for them—in white. They always did this, then painted their own faces white. These paintings are used only when the men are going to war.

The Giant, an ancestor of theirs, who was very large, told them to do this. He was later buried out here in the monte and his descendants say his bones were as big as a whale's. When Buro Alazan was a boy they took him to where the man was buried and showed him the remains of a skeleton lying on its back. The ribs were as big around as the spread of Buro's arms and bigger, and he had a wife and family who were just as large. The grave is on the point of the Playa near Ses ko see-et, the well where we get water.

This huge man was a great warrior, but he never fought with the Seris. He always fought alone. When he would pull his bow and let the string strike his wrist-guard just a little, it would sound like dynamite going off. He was as tall as a *sahuesa* giant cactus. If they met him in the monte he could pick up a man and carry him under his arm. If the man was bad he would break his arms and legs and leave him there, but he would never kill him.

One of the ordinary Seris challenged him to fight on the beach. They fought with bows and arrows; but, when the Seri shot, his arrow would not go into the giant. He was enormous and very ugly, and he tied his great knot of hair behind his head into a ball. A wasp built a nest in his hair. When he would get mad the wasps would come out and sting everybody. When the Seris saw that the Seri's arrow would not go into him, they all ran up the beach. The giant caught the Seri who had shot at him, stuck him under his arm and went off with him.

The Seris used to eat only sea food, but this giant ate only meat that he had killed in the monte. When he killed anybody he cut off the man's head and took it to his house in the brush. After the Seris had killed their enemies they would take their heads to their houses in the same way. They would build one big house and plant a tall pole in front of it and hang all the heads, one after the other, on the pole.

The giant never ate the flesh of his enemies. He

would drive live animals down to the shore here and kill them. He had so many in front of him he was like a rich man, with cattle and horses. They were like a herd of sea lions on the shore. One time he drove a lot to the shore and half of them went into the sea and swam across to the Island. They turned into fish, turtles and sea lions. To this day you can see the fur on the sea lion's back, such as they used to have when they were land animals. Of all the animals that swam to the Island there are left only the buro deer, the coyote and the jack rabbit—no cottontails, no wild hogs, no badgers.

The Seris went out to kill the giants only two or three times. They were very brave warriors, but they never killed any giants. Nobody knows how the giants died. Buro Alazan can show us their bones. There are two skeletons. It is thought they killed each other, although one is on one side of the sand-flat and the other on the other side, a mile or two away. But their arrows would reach across.

The giant carried in his hair over his temples a scorpion on each side, and when he wanted to fight he would make these *alacranes* bite him, to make him fierce. He would get so *bravo* that he didn't mind if they bit him all over the face—it would just make him braver.

He wore a long gown. Nobody knew what it was made of, but neither wind nor water could go through it. His hat was so big that six or seven men could not lift it. After he had fought a battle and was dancing, the women would gather to watch him. He was so enormous that one time he picked up a handful of women and put them in his sombrero. The only weapons he had or needed were his bow and arrows. He was a kind giant and would not kill the Seris. He would just break their arms and legs. He would never shoot them where it would kill them, but usually in the shoulder. Any one of the Seri warriors could have killed him, because many times they found him asleep in the monte, but they never did.

When the Mexicans began to come into this country with their animals and horses, the deer and game became scarce and the Seris got hungry. They found where, over the mountains, the horses went up to feed, and killed two of them. Then they ate all the meat they could and took the rest over to the Island.

The Government sent soldiers, and all the ranchers came out against them. They fought and the Seris killed two without losing any; and from then on there was always war, because the ranchers said the cattle and horses belonged to them. Another Government came in and a good Governor told them they could kill cattle and horses when they were hungry, or their women and children were hungry, but they must tell the nearest rancher so he could report to the Governor. Then there would be no fight. But some of the ranchers were very bad people. They told the Government that the Seris had killed horses when they had not, and then the fights began again.

The Seri warriors painted their faces for war. When they were so painted they could not feel pain or cold. It is a long time since the Seris have painted for war. In the cold weather the women paint their faces all over, so they will not feel the cold. The red and white colors are earths that they can get on the Island; also the blue, which comes from a plant as tall as a man, and has a very pretty flower. They grind the flower fine and mix it with stone and it makes blue.

If a woman has but one daughter, the girl paints her face like her mother. If she has more, they paint their faces with another pattern. After a battle the painting on their faces is different—one pattern if they lose and another if they win, but in any case the color is white.

If the warriors lose in battle and any Seris are killed, the women snatch the men's arrows out of their quivers and throw them away. They sit in a circle and cry and wail for four to six days. The Seris killed in battle are left where they fall, for the birds and buzzards to eat. Their bodies are of no value now. It is a long time since they have had any battles. The last man they killed was a white man who landed on Tiburon from a gasoline launch. He was killed by Buro's brother.

Since the Governor who told them they could kill cattle went away there has not been another Government like that. Even when they asked permission to kill a burro or a horse the ranchers got angry and drove them away. So the Seris tore up the paper they made with the good Government, because these Governments are all bad.

The old women generally paint their faces red like blood, but this is just to keep out the cold. The younger girls paint any pictures they like on their faces—different ones, just to make themselves pretty. The lines across the nose indicate their mother's family or clan. On the cheeks they can make something different.

When Buro Alazan was a little boy, his mother painted his face the same as hers—because he was her son. His father did not have the same marks on his face when he was painted—he painted his face only with the blood of an animal he had killed. When the women saw him coming back to camp they would see the paint and be happy. They would say:

"Look, he has killed!"

Then he would take a smear of blood from his face and put it on his bow. This meant: "I have killed a buro deer!" Or whatever animal it was. It was just a sign that he had killed.

Each family has a different painting. If a woman has children her family paints one kind of picture only. She can paint all her children, including the little boys, like herself; but afterwards all the daughters, except the oldest, can use any picture they want. If a girl is going to get married she paints her face different from her mother. She paints it very beautifully. After she is married she is not supposed to paint, but they do paint.

CHAPTER XVI

Buro Alazan Makes His Talk

THE information which Buro Alazan had been so anxious to impart turned out to be of real value, but I did not tell him so. I just let him go on, telling his stories in his own way, and when he stopped I gave him a peso. That was what he was really waiting for, and he grabbed it and left on the run for the bootlegger's house.

Ever since the Roosevelt yacht had steamed away, the fishermen had been doing a big business. The sea bass were running strong and, with the help of a few sticks of dynamite, they were bringing them in by the boatload. But as long as the trim yacht was in sight not a Mexican would put to sea, for it was currently believed it was a Government Patrol boat, come to arrest them for fishing without a license.

Now everything was wide open again, and a succession of mezcal peddlers kept the Indians on a continuous drunk. That was why Buro Alazan was so anxious to collect, he being still possessed of a man-size thirst but too old to earn money by fishing. It was to gratify this craving for the white man's fire-water that he and Juan Tomas' had rousted Santo Blanco out of his job—and already Juan Tomas' was down and out.

That afternoon Hampton went up to visit him, and we were just getting into our car to follow when he came hurrying back. He was followed by the wildest-looking Seri we had ever seen—just over from Tiburon

Island—and did not stop to explain anything. Snatching up his collecting kit he started off down the trail, leaving us to deal with this drunken savage, who was holding out his hand significantly.

"*Da me viente centavos!*" he said, and I could see he expected to get it. He had tagged along after Hampton for the better part of a mile—and twenty centavos was the price of a drink.

"Very well," I responded, picking up my camera. "Let me take your picture and I will pay you."

Twenty centavos was my established price whenever I photographed a Seri, although I could just as well have taken them for nothing. I have never seen Indians less camera-shy; but it is always best to pay. Then there can be no exorbitant demands later. A bargain has been made, the money has changed hands: and, if the Indian gets sick or is killed, there can be no charges of witchcraft or evil eye.

The wild man from Tiburon posed obediently and I gave him twenty centavos. Then, to show what a good sport I was—and to get him out of camp—I invited him to ride on my running-board and dropped him at the house of the amiable Mrs. Ugarte, where he could get quick action for his money. From there on it was sandy and we had to walk, but as we were strolling through the village the wild man caught up with us and passed his brawny left arm around my neck.

He had had one drink, but he wanted another one. "*Da me cigarros!*" he wheedled; and I could feel his arm contract. One quick squeeze, and a jerk from the other hand, and my neck would be broken. It was the particular way the Seris killed their enemies when they leapt on them while they slept, though I did not know it then.

"No," I said, "you have had enough *cigarros*, already!" *Cigarros* was their euphemism for a drink of mezcal, and I chose to take it as a joke. But he was very much in earnest.

"*Da me cigarros!*" he repeated and as he glared into my eyes I could see the other Seris looking scared. It was no joke to them, nor would it have been for me if the tribal matriarchs had not intervened. Their menfolks might be drunk, but they were not— and they could handle them, any time. Two of them rushed in and snatched his arm away, quickly bringing him to his senses with loud scolding. Then they dragged him off and I went on with my photography. But, after a reasonable interval, I left there and did not go back for several days. When an Indian gets drunk he reverts to the primitive savage, whose dominant urge is to kill.

One of the few sober men in camp was our little friend Santo Blanco, and he greeted us with a wan smile; but Buro Alazan had got his job away from him and was determined to keep it. At daylight the next morning Buro showed up for his breakfast, and whatever he said we took down. He chose, on this occasion, to correct Santo Blanco's version of the Creation; but so abysmal was his ignorance of tribal myth that he ran out of ideas in three sentences.

"The first Seri came from the point of Tiburon. First there was a man, and then a woman came to him. They had one child."

He paused then, to think the matter over and clear his muddled wits, and decided to talk about clothes.

All he could think of was material things—the dreamer had been left out of him entirely.

This first man came without clothes, said Buro, and he put on a sapeta—a gee-string. It was just to cover himself—he had no pantalones. Now even the little boys wear a sapeta. They made their clothing from the skins of animals. They softened the skins of the sea lion and pelican, but their gee-string they made of deerskin or rabbit-skin, which can be worked very soft. Later—when the Seris wore clothes—they threw them all away except their gee-string when they wanted to run fast.

They could run down a buro deer when they stripped for that purpose, and kill him without weapons by midday. Sometimes they would take a bow and arrows—no more—and, under their arm, their turtle-skin water bag.

At first the buro will run very fast. The Seris would pick out a very hot day, when the buro was full of mesquite beans; then they would go softly towards him and he would run. They would go to him again and he would run again. After a while he would only walk. Then they would run after him very fast and he would fall down with his tongue on the ground, and they could kill him with a stone or an arrow. Just when the sun rises the Seris creep up on a deer and scare him. Then follow him and, in the heat of the day, the buro will be so weak he will lie down. Then they grab him by the nose and horns and break his neck.

Buro's son, from the Island—the wild man who had followed Hampton to our camp and put his arm so lovingly around my neck—can still run them down.

This boy's name is Koi-air—I Hold Him In My Arms. That is the name his mother gave him when he was a baby. Now they call him Luis Torres. The Yaquis gave him that name, when they were putting in the boilers at Costa Rica Ranch, for Blevins.

When Buro was a child on the Island the Federal soldiers from Mexico City came and captured him and all his family and took them with many others to a little place this side of Pueblo de Seris, near Hermosillo, where they kept them a long time. The soldiers started a school and put Kolusio, a captured Seri, in charge of it. Kolusio had not been captured on the Island. He and Juan Antonio were Seris that used to go to Hermosillo to sell things, and they stayed with a Mexican family there.

Kolusio never came back to the Island, but Juan used to visit them in the cactus-pear season, to eat *pitahayas;* and in the turtle season, to eat *cahuamas.* Juan drank liquor all the time in Hermosillo; but Kolusio did not, because he feared the Government. He was the representative of the Seris at Hermosillo, and acted as schoolteacher and interpreter.

When they took all the Seris to Hermosillo and made them stay there, smallpox came and many of them died—grown ones and little ones and babies. So the rest of them ran away in the night and came back to the Island.

Four or five hundred Mexican soldiers went to fight the Yaquis who lived along the Yaqui River, and the Yaquis killed almost all of them. More soldiers came, in a long line. They had some cannon and the Yaquis could do nothing, because they would be dead before they got to the soldiers. Then the soldiers took many Yaquis prisoners and marched them to Hermosillo.

About fifteen Yaquis fled into this country, and they were killing cattle and horses while they were hiding. The Seris took a few over on the Island—six men and three women, with their children. A big ship came up from Guaymas and brought many Papago soldiers. Many more Federal soldiers came on horseback, from the mainland, to help them. The Papago soldiers searched the Island, killing men, women and children, and the Federal soldiers prevented the Indians from escaping. Almost everybody was killed— but a few hid and escaped. The few families that they captured they took back to Hermosillo. Rafael Ysabel was the Governor at that time and General of the soldiers. He was a very bad man and killed all the women and children. They stabbed the babies with their swords.

When the ranchers first came into the country the Seris were friendly with them and made an agreement not to kill their cattle and horses without telling them. After Ysabel had killed nearly all their women and children, he sent word to the Seris to come in and make another treaty. But the old men said: "No!" and tore up the paper and threw it to the wind. Yesterday some cattle came close to the Seris' camp and the young men wanted to kill a cow, but they remembered their agreement and did not. It is the paper that Juan Tomas', the former chief, carries around his neck. It was made in 1911 and since then the Seris have never killed any cattle or horses without permission.

Chico Romero, the present chief, has a paper signed by Rodolfo Calles, the Governor, when he was head of the Council for the State of Sonora, and the paper is all stamped and sealed. It says that Chico Romero is known as the chief of the Seris and is to maintain order and cleanliness in his camp and is to give advice to the Government when any vessel touches at the Island. But Chico never goes to see the Government. Roberto Thompson, the half-American Mexican who is *Jefe de Vigilancia,* just comes down and visits the Seris, but gives them nothing.

When Juan Tomas' went up to Hermosillo and made a paper with the Government, this Government and two others gave the men sacks of flour and beans and cloth, knives, buckets and harmonicas. Big blankets, too—but since Chico Romero has been chief, the Seris have received nothing. They are very poor, and when the men and women go to Hermosillo they get nothing there. Chico stays drunk in town and never goes in the Government House. He does not speak for them—he just stays drunk. When Americans come down to visit them, Thompson sometimes comes with them, but just comes—he has no authority over the Seris.

Chico Romero's father was Juan Chavez. The Government took Juan away, with his wife and five other men and women, and they never came back. This was to punish them for killing some Americans. Three Americans landed on the Island and gave the Seris all kinds of presents. They were good men, but the Seris' Governor was a bad man; and, after all this, he secretly told his men to kill them. The boat was very beautiful—white with a flag of red, blue and white on a very tall mast.

The Seri women cried out: *"Pobrecitos!"* and said it was a shame to kill the Americans. But their chief ordered the men to, so they killed them. This was about sixty years ago, when Buro was a small boy.

One American escaped, two were killed. Then the Government came and took six men and four women away and they have never come back. Before Buro was born, an American was killed near Tepoca, but he is the only other one the Seris have killed.

The Seris used to have a medicine for rattlesnake bite, but now they have not. It was made of hediondia —creosote bush. They still know how to make this medicine, but it does not work. Many women get bitten while out hunting cactus-pears and they find them dead three or four days later, eaten up by coyotes. When the people see bitten folks' legs begin to swell up they all begin to cry.

A long time ago the Seris had two wives. Porfirio Diaz, the old man who lives in the last house in the village, used to have two wives, but now he has none. He is old. He has a great many daughters. There is a family up the Coast where a man has two wives.

If a man is married, all the women object if he wants to take another woman. They never let him have two women together, but sometimes a man has a woman here and another one who lives away up the Coast. For a long time the men have not had two wives; but when they did, if the wives ever came together, there was a fight right then.

Nacho Romero tried to have two wives, but the women took one of them away from him. Now she is alone—Ramona. The women all got angry, so the girl's father, Santo Blanco, took her away from Nacho. Santo Blanco is smaller than Chico and not rich. He is just a fisherman. The woman now has a baby. She lives with her mother in one part of the village and Nacho lives farther up.

If a girl wants to get married and the rest of the

women agree, she can get married. If they object, she cannot. If a girl and a man want to be married, he will have to have quite a lot of goods.

There are unmarried women among the Seris now who do not want to get married. Santo Blanco has three daughters who are old enough to marry, but they will not. Chico has one the same. Candelaria is now getting to be an old woman, and many men have wanted to marry her. But she drinks a great deal, and now none of the men want her. Because in the night she drinks and goes back and forth drunk. None of these women, no matter how drunk, ever have intercourse with men. No man wants to marry Ramona now, because she gets drunk and has a bad temper. Greek Pete, who works in the store, tries to get the Seri women but they will have nothing to do with him.

CHAPTER XVII

Seri War Stories

SPEAKING of Greek Pete—who kept the store for
Corona and was a villainous-looking rascal—
made Buro Alazan think of money and what it would
buy, and he paused and looked up expectantly. So I
gave him his peso and he left in a hurry, well-satisfied
he had got the best of me. But from this gossip of the
village I had got a new insight into the loves and
hates of his people and I was satisfied to have him
continue.

He was a typical old Seri and a war chief of re-
nown, and his version of Ramona's sad romance gave
another aspect to the affair. It was colored, of course,
by his hatred of Santo Blanco. But I was getting the
real low-down on the morals of these younger women
who had set up to be modern "flappers." But the three
daughters of Santo Blanco were very quiet and modest, and I knew Buro was lying about them.

Like most old soldiers fighting their battles over,
Buro made much of the Seri victories, and the injus-
tices which they suffered, saying nothing of their de-
feats. One of the greatest of these, according to an
American who had been a leader in the pursuit, was
when the Seris escaped in the night and fled from
their camp near Hermosillo. This was after the Mexican Government had rounded them up and moved
them to a ranch west of town, where they were supposed to learn civilized ways. But one morning the

encampment was found empty and an armed party
followed after them.

As the Seris came to the playa west of Kino Bay,
Buro Alazan and his followers kept on up the beach;
but Juan Tomas', the senior war chief, laid an ambush
on the edge of the wide flat and, when the posse was
out in the open, they opened fire with what guns they
had. But their aim was poor, none of the pursuers was
hurt; and, when they charged in, the Seris fled to the
edge of the water. When this American and the others
closed in, to take them prisoners, the Indians plunged
into the Gulf and began to swim towards the Island,
which was many miles away.

In order to turn them back from their suicidal attempt this American began to shoot in front of them;
but the Seris, thinking he was trying to kill them,
kept on till some few reached Tiburon. Among these
was old Juan Tomas', but both his wives perished in
the attempt, along with most of the women and children. The people who had followed Buro Alazan escaped up the beach and took shelter on the Island.

Another story, told by Corona, is of three Papago
brothers who were killed in a Seri attack; and of their
sister's plot for revenge. Going to Hermosillo she
complained to the Government of their death and
offered, if they would send soldiers, to lead them
across the channel on dry ground. Then, after con-
sulting the tide tables, the expedition set out and, on
the night of a very low tide, the cavalry rode across
the strait.

All the Seris were living along the beach and the
soldiers, riding both ways, attacked their camps, driv-
ing the survivors in terror into the interior. Then, taking advantage of the low tide the next day, they

crossed back to the mainland again. Many Indians were killed in this surprise attack, and for a long time the Seris were afraid, especially at very low tides. Buro had plenty of other stories to tell, and the next morning he continued his tales.

When Buro Alazan was small he went with his father up to the water at the big Red Mountain. At that time his father wore only a gee-string and so did he. They carried food with them for eight days. When they came to where some Seris were fishing, far to the north, they found some Papagos who acted very friendly. But Buro's father overheard the Papagos talking bad, so he took him back to the Island.

The next night one hundred and sixty Seris—all warriors, no women or young men—talked all night. The next day everybody, including the young men, began making arrows, until many quivers were filled. In the night all the men went across to the mainland; but they kept away from the waterside and the next night they saw many fires at Puerto Posado. Then the scouts came back and said:

"There are more Papagos than Seris."

When the sun rose the Seris attacked the Papagos, who were not prepared, and they killed so many of their enemies that few escaped back to their homes. Many Seris were killed. Manuel Molino, the brother of Porfirio Diaz, had an arrow pass entirely through him, but he did not die. He killed many Papagos and lived a long time afterwards, until he was finally killed by some vaqueros.

After the battle, in which many Seris were killed, the rest retreated to the Island. The Mexicans captured all the women, but they let them go again. One said that, since so many men have been killed, they

might as well let the women go back to the Island.
Buro's brother was shot through the arm, and Buro
got one bullet through his left arm and could not hold
his bow to shoot. Some of the Seris deserted the ones
who were fighting. The man who led them away had
been shot through the neck. When he drank water it
would run down outside, but he did not die.

Before Buro was born his father used to go to the
mainland of Lower California to hunt sea lions and
turtles, and to gather a different kind of maguey.
Since then the Seris have never been across the Gulf,
although they have boats now. His father met people
over there whose language was no good. They could
make noises, but they could not talk. Their noise was
like a coyote. When they saw the Seris coming in
their balsas they all ran away. There were no canoes
in those days.

When these strange people saw them going out on
the water in their balsas they were afraid. They had
no boats for hunting, but used to spear seals off the
rocks, and catch young ones which they traded to the
Seris, who tanned their hides. These little seals were
spotted, like a scorpion. All the people used to go to
the southeast point of the Island to see them put off
and come back. One time, when they were coming
back, the Seris found a large barque off the point. The
people on it gave them presents. When the people on
shore saw these presents a great many of them went
aboard the ship, and it took them all down to Guaymas
—men, women and children.

When those that were left saw them sail away they
sent men down the Coast, to watch where the ship
went. One of the men followed them clear to Guaymas. Other Indians who lived there told him they had

been shut up in a big house. The Seris watched it, and one night the prisoners escaped and they all went home through the brush. No one was killed. The Government caught all the Seris they could and took them to Guaymas. The boys were put in one place, the girls in another.

Another time the soldiers came by land and got them. They did not put them in a house, but they kept them guarded—this side of Pueblo de Seris, near Hermosillo. They had no house there, but lived beside big trees, and a man with a book talked to them. After a while a few Seris escaped and joined those who were watching outside—and then more escaped, until the soldiers had none left.

Buro's brother was taken to Mexico City by President Porfirio Diaz. He never came back, but a big, black ship returned and passed through the straits between San Estevan and the Island, very slowly. It had a white flag and a very tall mast, but the Seris would not go aboard.

Juan Tomas', the old war chief.

All men, when they are children, are given a baby name by their mother—Juan's was Ich ah payt'. They receive another name when they grow up. Before Juan Tomas' became chief, Buro's father and Juan's mother were joint governors. Buro's grandfather was Manuel Miranda. Juan Tomas' lived at Tepoca; but when he was a young man, Miranda took him to the Island and made him Chief. Juan Tomas' is not an ancient chief, but of late times. He is the oldest man among the Seris—said to be over a hundred years old.

Miranda never had any battles, either with the

Government or with the other Indians. He was very peaceful and the people who died, died because they were sick. He was a good Governor. Many times he went to the Government and they gave him presents; and always, when he came back, everything he brought was divided evenly among all the tribe, and he kept nothing.

Juan Tomas' used to do the same thing when he was chief. When Chico goes to town he just gets drunk, and anything he gets at any time he keeps for himself. When they come back, there are always fights between Chico and his three brothers, and his brothers always whip him. They don't stop beating him until the people pull them off. Santo Blanco and Chico are always starting a fight, too, but the people stop them.

The people did not want Chico for Governor—they wanted Juan Tomas' to keep on. But the two Thompson brothers made Chico Governor. They took Chico to the Mexican Governor at Hermosillo and had him made chief, without taking Juan Tomas'' paper away from him.

The Government has told the Seris not to allow people to go on the Island, either Mexicans or Americans; but Thompson told Chico to take *his* friends over free—then he could charge all the others five pesos and keep the money for himself. Chico is a bad *hombre*. He has three brothers—Jose, Nacho and Roberto. Manuel Encinas' son is a policeman—a good man. He never gets into trouble when he goes to Hermosillo.

When Juan Tomas' was young, Buro was a warrior under him. At that time they had been left without a government, because the old chief had been killed by some ranchers, when he was asleep. So Juan Tomas'

led them. Buro and Juan Tomas' were down at Tastiota when the Chief was killed, and Juan led them to
fight the Yoris who had killed their Chief.

The father of Santo Blanco wanted to be Chief, but
when he went to Libertad, Andreas Noriega, the Mexican rancher there, killed him. The Seris had been to
Hermosillo to buy mezcal and had brought back many
bottles, which they sold to the Mexicans for clothes
and serapes. The Mexicans at Libertad Ranch, where
they were building a house for Andreas, all got drunk;
and he got drunk, too. At night the Seris lay down
beside the fire and Andreas came out and said:

"Give me a cigarette!"

When a man got up to give him one Andreas shot
him and he fell into the fire, dead. It was Santo
Blanco's father.

The soldiers came and took Andreas to prison in
Hermosillo; and, before they let him out, the Government took away everything he had—his land, his cattle, his gold. His gold was in a big box. Buro was at
Libertad working for Andreas when they sent word
to dig up the box, which was buried in the big room.
They took it to Hermosillo, and one man could not
carry it. After four months they let Andreas out.
When he got out he did not have a centavo left.

After this Juan Tomas' went to Hermosillo and got
a good paper for Governor or Capitan. This side of
Puerto Libertad the Seris were fishing when some
Mexicans came, and Juan Tomas' went over to beg for
a cigarette. When he was a few feet away the Mexicans shot at him and Juan Tomas' fell forward and
broke his thumb. The bullet did not hit him—it was
just that he had been shot before, and the bullet had
injured his hand.

When Juan Tomas' was small there was a feud between his brothers and some other Seris. The three brothers went to kill one of the men, but he killed all three of them. Juan Tomas' was then fighting with his bow and arrow and got a bullet from a muzzle-loading gun through his left hand, which was bad for a long time so he could not draw a bow. When he grew older he took a cap-and-ball gun and shot the man who had killed his brothers. Buro knew Juana Maria, the famous Elder-woman of the Turtle Clan —and her mother, Jacinta, who was head woman before her. Juana Maria's mother was painted the same as she was—with white lines, like a man—but *her* daughter, Candelaria, was painted pretty. There are no women now who paint as pretty as she did, and there is no woman in the tribe now who bosses the other women like Juana Maria. Candelaria would never marry and is big and fat now.

When the Seris visit a place like Costa Rica Ranch, only the women and children would go—together with the young men who were serving their families, to bring water and carry wood, and who were going to marry their daughters. These boys would build the houses, which were the property of the women of the family. No man could work at this building except the young men who had to bring wood and water. The houses were not very good, because they would only stay a short time.

The man has nothing to say about the house—it is the property of the woman only. When the house is finished she builds a fire by the door. Then the man can come in and sit on her left side, while the children sit on her right-hand side.

She feeds her man first, then the children. Some-

times she gives the little children a very little food,
when they have gone for water or for wood and come
back tired. The woman eats last. Now, in Buro's
house, it is different, because he has no children. He
has had two wives—the first died. His second wife is
the widow of El Mashem, the Seri interpreter, but
she is not the mother of Buro's sons. His first wife was
Rosa. By her he had seven sons, but they all died except one—and he has one daughter. All his present
wife has are her grandchildren. So in feeding them it
is not the same. When the grandchildren are hungry
she feeds them first.

Angelita is the wisest *bruja*, or witch woman, in the
tribe. She is the daughter of Francisco Molino. She
can chew one piece of meat and take it out of her
mouth and it is yellow. The next mouthful will be
red. It is very pretty to watch her make the food come
out of her mouth in different colors.

Buro's grandson, Jesus Feliz, knows more about the
gods than anybody. He can do magic, and goes up to
the caves. He can take a broken plate, such as they
have in Hermosillo, put it on the fire in the cave, and
lead to make bullets will come out of it. When he
wants powder he picks up a handful of sand and lets it
run between his fingers. That which falls on the
broken plate is powder—strong, black powder.

The mouth of the cave is very narrow and a man
cannot go in. It looks just like the wall of a house.
There is no hole—it is hard rock. He takes his knife
and sticks it into the rock. Then he can walk in, where
it is white, like the Church in Hermosillo. No man's
knife can go into Feliz's body—it just bends.

Jesus Feliz is not old, but he is getting blind already. He goes around with his eyes half-closed.

When he is going to the cave he does not eat food or drink water for four days. During these four days he never leaves his little house. He stays only one day in the cave. When he is leaving the cave he swings a bull-roarer around, so the spirits will not come out. Manuel Encinas knows the witches very well, too. When he goes to the cave he takes that thing that makes a loud noise, the bull-roarer—and when he gets near he swings it and the spirits come.

CHAPTER XVIII

Last Talk of Buro Alazan

WE CUT short our stories of warriors and witches to take some medicine to Juan Tomas, who was reported very low. The old man was lying, coiled up in the sand like a dog, by the door of his daughter's house; but when Americano rubbed the ointment on his chest he roused up and asked for something to eat. His daughter brought him out a can of flour gruel, made exactly like the paste that a paper hanger uses, only containing more and larger lumps. It is the favorite civilized food of the Seris, especially when sweetened with *panoche*—simply flour stirred into hot water and made into a sort of mush.

One dose of this terrible compound would just about finish off a white man, but the Seris have a digestion which balks at nothing, as they had demonstrated only a few months before. The retiring manager of the hunting Lodge, who did not love them too much, had paid them for their last job with a collection of badly spoiled canned goods. These cans had gone through the tremendous heat of summer and were swelled up almost to bursting, but the Indians emptied them all in one grand fiesta and came back to ask for more.

So, to Juan Tomas', this flour paste was quite a delicacy, although it did not bring him out of his weakness. His broken ribs had not knit together, and made it difficult for him to breathe. To us he seemed in the last stages of pneumonia, and the Indians were very grave. They had stopped, at last, their mad round of drinking as they realized what it had done to their old Chief—and, sometime in the night, he died. When Americano called the next morning the body had been spirited away and buried, and every house in that end of the village was being torn down.

A line had been drawn just east of Juan Tomas'' house and all the west end of the camp was deserted, the Indians moving across the line. On every brush hut a white flag had been raised, and from time to time the women would burst out wailing. Yet there were those in the village who were reconciled to his passing and Santo Blanco seemed quite serene. The body of his old enemy had been hidden in the sand-hills and, after four days, his spirit would either ascend to heaven or remain, an unlovely ghost, to terrify the people with its outcries. In any case he would not return corporeally, to drive Santo Blanco away from our tent, and the next morning he was back for breakfast.

Buro Alazan had arrived before him and, while they were filling up on white man's food, they bandied words defiantly. But Buro was now in a more subdued frame of mind and, after a particularly snappy come-back from Santo Blanco, he relapsed into a sullen silence. But that did not keep him from reporting for duty; and Santo Blanco, after giving me a small present, smiled knowingly and went away.

As long as vindictive old Juan Tomas' had been behind him, Buro Alazan had felt sure of his job; but now, after four days of war stories and the chit-chat of the village, he was beginning to run out of material. Either that or Santo Blanco had buffaloed him, for he started off rather weakly with the story of the Big Coyote.

A long time ago, he said, there used to be an animal
called a coyote. He was very big and very brave. He
would come close to where the Seris lived, and was not
afraid; but the Seris were afraid of him, even the
warriors. When he would throw up his head his hair
was bushy, like that of Juan Tomas', and he made a
noise like many coyotes. All the warriors would shoot
arrows at him, but he stood still—and the arrows
would drop to the ground. He would not go near the
water. Every night the women were afraid of him
because he had killed a woman and her child. Though
the women told the men to kill him, they could not.

After he had killed many people, one Seri said he
would kill Coyote. He stood at the edge of the rocks,
where the channel past the Island is wide. When the
Coyote came, the man threw down his quiver and bow
and leapt into the sea. Coyote sprang after him. The
man swam on top and under, like a sea lion, and
the coyote followed him—until he was away out from
land and drowned. The man swam back.

After telling this story, Buro paused and sat brood-
ing a while. Then he roused up and continued with
his tales.

The Big Black Turtle is called *mos-neh ih pohl.* He
understands the Seri language. When they spear him
they say: "You take me home." He turns toward the
shore and they say: "My family is waiting for you."
If he does not head straight for the shore they tell him
and he goes straight. When they get close to the shore
they point out which is their home and he goes there.
Buro does not eat him, because he is a Seri. His meat
is dark, like horse meat.

When they get to land the man tells him to turn
over on his back. He puts his flapper in the sand and

turns himself over and lays his head on the ground. Then they kill him and eat him. He lives on the west side of the Island. He does not lay his eggs on the beach, but in the sand dunes. He lays a great many eggs and covers them up. He is longer than a man, and wider than a man can reach. He is the only animal that can understand Seri. When they steer him and he is heading out to sea they tell him he is going the wrong way. He must turn around and take them back to their families. So he turns around and takes them home.

There is a Big Snake in the high mountains on Tiburon—more than one. They are as big around as this tent—ten feet in diameter. When he crawls along, squirming, he moves rocks which roll down the mountain, and he crushes trees with the weight of his body. He eats buro and venado deer, but not their horns. When he gets close to where there is a buro he does not catch him with his mouth but with his tail—he hooks him in. The buro cannot run, because the snake is stronger than a whale with its breath. It just opens its mouth and sucks him in.

When the Seris see a big snake they run like the devil. No one ever tried to kill one. They live up on the high mountain and the Seris are afraid to go there. Sometimes when they are hunting buros they see one, but they always run. The snakes have never eaten any Seris.

The Whale is big, but he has no teeth and never hurts the Seris. They never hurt him, but if a whale dies they eat him. He is very good and the fat is like that of beef.

Buro's grandson can take sand in his hand, hold it a minute, and when he throws it in the fire it will blow up like powder. He has a broken plate from Hermosillo from which he can get lead to make bullets. He learns these things when he goes to the Holy Cave. He leaves his house at sunset, after four days without food or drink, and walks all night till he gets to the cave. When the sun comes up he goes into the cave, which he has opened with his knife. He lies down for four days and neither eats nor drinks, and he learns these things from a spirit that is in the cave. For two days after he gets back he does not speak but drinks a little water, and on the third day he eats a little food. On the fourth day all the people come around and bring him much food. They have a fiesta. He sings to them new songs about what happened in the cave, and they are all very happy.

There is a girl, Angelita, who does the same thing. When she comes back they have a big dance and sing all night. She is the daughter of Petra, the old blind woman.

A long time ago a white man came to the Island in a boat and all the men met him—there was no woman present. At that time they had two chiefs, Francisco Molino and Juan Tomas', and Molino was in charge on the Island. This man landed and gave them shirts and some smokes. They all crowded around him. Then one of the men said: "Let's kill him!"

They opened fire on him with guns and he fell, but he held onto the side of the boat. Then he fired back and killed one Seri. The Seris all ran to where their women were, up on the mountain. They came back the next morning and found the white man dead. He had been shot through the stomach, twice through the head and once through the arm. They dragged him out on the sand. Antonio Aguilar, who was the biggest man in size in the tribe, was very angry because they had killed the white man; and, though the others of the tribe wanted to kill some more Yoris, Molino stopped them. Buro's son got this man's Mauser rifle and has it yet. Buro's rifle was full of cartridges when he commenced shooting. When he stopped there was only one left.

Long afterwards the Government at Guaymas sent a boat up. The trouble had started because some Mexican fishermen came to the Island and killed some Seris. That is why they killed the white man.

Buro Alazan seemed to realize that he had gone a little too far in admitting he had helped to kill this white man; and, after thinking a while, he spoke briefly on less dangerous matters.

This is Buro Alazan's arrow mark. It proves his right to any game he kills and is the same sign the Navajos use for rain—two half moons. His father taught him to shoot. He made him a little bow with small arrows, and taught him to shoot at running lizards and little birds on bushes. They call this arrow mark their *fierro*, or iron—it is like a cow-brand. He can shoot an arrow a hundred meters on the level, and further if he points it up. When he was younger he could shoot about one hundred and fifty meters, and he is a good bowman yet.

But arrows were no good to kill Mexicans with, because the vaqueros would fall over on the further side of their horses and the arrow would just hit the ani-

mal. If they shoot a buro standing the arrow goes
clear through him; if running, it just sticks out on
the other side.

One time there were two families camped at Tecomate Spring, in the northeast corner of Tiburon.
They walked around like other people all day, and
were not sick. When night came they went to sleep
close to a water-hole and the next morning one family
found all five of the others dead, just as they had gone
to sleep. Now the Seris never sleep near a water-hole,
but as far away as the sand hills, about half a mile.

The devil that lives in Tecomate Spring is like an
animal. He is in all springs. He lives also in mesquite
and ironwood trees. The Seris never sleep under a big
tree, because they are afraid of these animals. The
devil lies invisible at the bottom of the spring all day,
and comes out at night. He also lives under the roots
of giant cacti, and any big tree.

The spirits in caves are good and do not do harm.
They live in wells, too. Manuel Encinas has seen them
—he can talk with the spirits and animals. He can
take a section of cane, hold it up in the air, and talk to
the spirits; and, when you take the cane, white powder
will pour out—or blue—whatever color he says. It is
good medicine. When a person is very sick they send
for Manuel, and he brings some of this good medicine.
He looks into their bodies and, wherever he finds the
sickness, he puts a cross with this white powder. Then
he puts little crosses, one on each side of the nose. If he
does that, people won't die. It is long since Manuel
went to the cave. When he was a boy he went often.
Now he is deaf.

They are all called Seris now; but there are some,
like this Juan up at Tepoca, who have lived among the

Tepocas and the Tastioteñas. The Tepocas and Tastioteñas were different tribes once, but the Seris finished
them all off. The Tepocas used to speak Papago. The
Seris used to intermarry with the Tepocas. One time
a young girl of Tiburon married a young man who
came from Tepoca. And one time a young man from
the Island married a widow of the Tepocas, who had
a big house. They never married with the Tastioteñas.
These people cannot speak Seri or Yori—just their
own language. They are very far off—down the
Coast.

"Five years and this one ago," said Buro, "a big
sickness came and killed more Seris than are now living.
When it came I went out of my house and the sickness
came after me, and I went to the Island—to the far-
off western shore. I stayed outside—did not go into a
house—and in the daytime walked far. The sickness
did not follow me."

The sickness was only among the Seris on the mainland. When it got them, they choked and died. Buro's
wife was sick when he left, but he took her with him
and she got well. His nieces and cousins died—there
were thirty-three died on the mainland shore. The
Seri fishermen who came here from the Island died.

It is said—Buro does not know if it is true—that
the families of Seris who lived at Tastiota many years
ago had saltworks and used to sell salt. They would
get in exchange calves, cows, colts and young mares,
and they built themselves a big house. They all lived
together. They had flour, and they had corn and meat
and chili and blankets, because they sold this salt.

The people there were Seris, but they did not go to
the Island. They learned to work, but the Island Seris
did not. In those days the Seris used to visit Hermosillo,

as they did later under Juan Tomas'. When the tribe
was in need, Juan Tomas' would lead all the men,
women and children into town, and the Government
would give them presents.

Now, with Chico, it is just the same as not having
any Government. He never punishes anybody when
they fight with knives and clubs and kill each other.
Nor does he go to the Government at Hermosillo, to
get provisions. He is one of the worst of all of them,
because he is drunk more than any. When Tomas' was
Governor he never got drunk, although he drank a
little. But they would always obey him, and what he
told them to do was always good. Francisco Molino,
when he was co-Governor, was the same as Juan
Tomas' and the people obeyed him. Chico is drunk all
the time, and when he gives orders no one obeys him.

Now all the young men are learning to speak Spanish. They are no good. In the old days they did not
know how to read and write and speak to the Yoris,
but they were well and strong and had plenty to eat,
and the people in Hermosillo gave them clothes to
wear. The young men now may be healthy, but they
are not good men.

Santo Blanco is another bad one. He is always making trouble, like Chico Romero. He is very jealous and
causes fights. He is Buro's first cousin on his mother's
side. It was Santo Blanco's father, Pancho Noriega,
who led most of the attacks where Yoris were killed.
He used to be Governor, and under him three Seri
men and one old woman were killed by the Mexicans,
but he did nothing. He fought with the Yoris, but he
was not much good.

Now that Juan Tomas' is gone, Santo Blanco wants
to be Governor, but none of the Seris want him. He is

loco, and when he gets drunk he is very ugly. There are only three good men left, Porfirio Diaz, Urbano Sanchez, and Ramon Montaño, Buro's son-in-law. Buro's son, Luis Torres, is also a good worker. He behaves himself and, though he does get a little drunk, he never gets angry. But he would be no good for Governor, because he works for his own family all the time.

One of the Seris at Tastiota had cattle and horses and became a great chief, because during the trouble among the Seris he stole the ranchers' cattle and ran off the colts and horses. His name was Francisquillo. He had two grown sons with families, and they helped him steal. The Government sent soldiers and caused him a great deal of trouble, on account of the killing of cattle. His own sons at last captured their father and tied his little fingers together with wire. Then they gave him to the soldiers, who took him to Hermosillo and executed him.

Juana, the wife of Porfirio Diaz, has horses on the Island now. She bought a mare from the Santa Maria Ranch the other day, but before they could take it to the Island the dogs scared it and it ran away. The Seris could not catch it alive, so they killed it and ate it.

To get the horses to the Island they tie all their feet together and put them on their backs in a boat. Juana has one stallion on the Island and two mares, which will have colts in the spring. The other Seris do not kill her horses. They·have been hungry, but they do not eat them. Five of the Seris are now preparing to buy horses and take them to the Island.

Porfirio Diaz' wife, Juana, got the money to buy her horses by working for Jim Blevins; husking corn

and gathering beans for one peso a day. Four other
Seris were working for him and they all earned a dollar a day. That's why she has so much money.

The woman paid twenty-five pesos for her first
horse, but Jim Blevins sold her the second mare for
ten pesos. Mexican fishermen have tried to shoot the
mares, but if they do the Seris will kill them. Five
years ago some Mexicans went to the Island, and one
of the Seri boys was in the mountains, hunting for
honey. Later the Seris found where a Mexican had
shot him. The man who killed him is here in Kino
Bay.

Roberto Estroga is the name of the big young man
they call El Vaquero. He can ride a bronk like a Mexican. He is the son of Buro's brother, Manuel Molino.
Pedro Mendez is Buro's son-in-law. He is here for the
fishing, but as soon as it is over he will go back to the
Island and not come back for a long time. He will
spear turtles and dry the meat.

All the morning it became increasingly evident that
Buro Alazan was running out of material. I had engaged him to talk for a week, but in five days he had
told all he knew. Having maligned the character of
Santo Blanco all he could, and given all his friends a
boost, he stopped short and held out his hand. But,
when I gave him a peso, the grouch he had been nurs-
ing came out.

"You give Santo Blanco a peso and a half!" he complained. And then I knew what Santo Blanco had told
him, when he had shut him up at breakfast. He had
informed the arrogant warrior that he was working
for less money than he himself had received. This was
the slow poison that had been eating at his heart, and
I could see he was ready to quit. But Santo Blanco, by

bringing me a present, had indicated that all was forgiven and he was ready to come back to work. So I admitted that I had paid Santo Blanco more. "Because he is a medicine man," I said. And the old chief stalked off in a huff.

CHAPTER XIX

"The Happy Song"

THIS conflict between the warrior class and the priesthood has been going on for centuries; but, intellectually, Buro was no match for the little man he had maneuvered out of his job. Santo Blanco had come back at him and so touched his pride that the slow-witted old war chief had quit.

If I had thought that Buro Alazan had anything more to contribute I might have raised *his* pay, but he was through and he knew it. He had dramatized his exit by a strike for higher wages, and I let him get away with it. But, if I now tried to hire back Santo Blanco immediately, he would realize how much I needed him; so, with Red Hat, I took a walk along the beach as a sign to all the world that we had quit.

For several days the weather had been stormy and threatening; and, if it ever did rain, we would be storm-bound at Kino Bay with no chance of getting away. The desert silt would turn into mud that would bog a pelican; and it was the part of wisdom, if we were going at all, to go now. We were seriously discussing such a move as we strolled along the windy shore when who should come in with a boatload of fish but Santo Blanco himself!

His wife and family, running down to meet him, stopped to greet us as we passed; and, busy as he was, Santo Blanco must have read our minds. He must have sensed that we were planning to go, for as we returned towards camp he came running after us with a model of a balsa he had made. It was four or five feet long, slenderly built of *carrizo* canes, and with the miniature figure of a hunter at the paddle, with his fishing spear and rope, complete. It even had a tiny olla to hold water and a mast to support the sail—all made to scale.

Knowing Santo Blanco as I did, I could hardly believe that this was intended for a gift; but he placed it in my hands with such a friendly smile that I almost thought it was. But, whether he was bringing it as a farewell present or building up on a sales campaign, we could not help but admire the graceful little boat, especially as it had been built by a savage. To construct a model, complete in every part, calls for a very nice sense of proportion; but for an Indian, whose people still lived in the Stone Age, it was a truly remarkable performance. So I took a chance and praised it first, before I asked if it was for me.

"Yes!" he answered. "Six pesos!"

Well, that was more like it! But how to get it home —through the threshing brush of the ironwoods and the bumps and chucks of the road!

"Five pesos!" he suggested, hopefully; and I weakened and gave him the five. It was only Mexican money, three pesos for a dollar; and, after he had worked so hard to make it, we could hardly refuse to buy.

He thanked us and, while the Seris gathered around to admire the tiny craft, a man offered to sell us his knife. It was a murderous-looking weapon, the blade made of an old ax-head, beaten out cold by many hours of pounding on the smooth rocks of Tiburon Beach. This Seri was a huge fellow, just over from the Island, and we gave him the peso he asked. Then, as

we bore our plunder to camp, a group of Indians followed us, each holding out something to sell.

Whatever it was, we took it and paid their price for
it, and the word must have spread that we were leaving, for just at dusk the wild man came. The same
rude barbarian who had slipped his arm around my
neck and murmured: *"Da me viente centavos!"*

But this time he was sober and, from a match-case
made of two cartridges, he poured out two black pearls.
Already he had offered them to Americano at the
Lodge, but had been unable to make a sale. Well,
Hampton knew pearls; but these, while small, were
perfectly formed, so we ventured to ask the price. The
wild one thought a minute, his glazed eyes fixed upon
me, just a suggestion of mezcal on his breath.

"Peso y medio!" he said at last.

A peso and a half was certainly not much for two
such beautiful black pearls, but with a man like him
it was necessary to drive a hard bargain or he would
be back with something more. Like a Shylock I demanded the match-case to boot, and he handed it over
with a sigh. To him those two empty cartridges that
fitted into each other were worth more than the pearls,
but he was perishing for a drink.

Since the death of Juan Tomas', the Kino Bay Seris
had suddenly sobered up. It was only these wild ones
from the Island who were selling their treasures to
buy mezcal. But the next morning, early, Santo Blanco
appeared with something else to sell. It was a dainty
little jug—a miniature olla—and in a long conversa-
tion after breakfast, he informed me it was used in
their weddings. Yes, indeed, it had great value; but
for me it would be only one peso.

"But," I objected, "this is no good to me unless I know the ceremony that goes with it."

" 'Sta bueno"—and he smiled—"I will tell you."

Thus it was that Santo Blanco edged back into his old job, and he stayed with it to the end. Every day until we left he told of greater signs and wonders, to induce me to remain; and, since it was money he was after, I dug up my bag of silver and filled all my pockets with pesos. What to me were a few dollars more or less, compared to the stories he could tell? But first of all—to make good on my bluff—I demanded the Marriage Ceremony.

"When a man and woman get married, a new basket, or a pot like this, is made. Then atole, or porridge, is made of eelgrass seeds and put into it. This basket or pot must be very pretty. The seeds of the *cholla* cactus are also put into the porridge. The mother and her daughter sit in the doorway of the young couple's new house and the mother gives the daughter food. *She* takes a clamshell and puts it beside her own, for the man. Then he comes. She gives him the shell of food. When he is through eating he takes water from a very small olla and rinses out his mouth. Then he drinks, a very little. Now they are married."

The small olla I had bought was one of these drinking cups, and I remarked on the fact that this marriage was very similar to that of the Navajos. They too, eat *atole* from the same basket and drink from a common cup. They also have a custom that, after the wedding, the man can never look his mother-in-law in the face again. Santo Blanco's eyes brightened and he said that that was their custom, too. Or it had been in the earlier days. Now, when they get old, they can look at each other. After they have had four children they can look at their mothers-in-law. In olden times the mother could never see her daughter after she was married. Now she cannot look at her daughter until a month after she is married—and the girl cannot look at her mother for two days and nights after she is married. When these have passed, the man brings food to his mother-in-law and they can look at each other. This is a very interesting parallel, though similar taboos are found among many primitive people in other parts of the world.

I asked if the Seris had coyote stories, like the Indians further north, and Santo Blanco identified three which they have in common with the Navajos:

1—Coyote wanted to marry his own daughter, so he courted her in the night when he would not be recognized, and gave her a jack rabbit not to tell.

2—Coyote saw the chickadees playing ball on a tree by throwing their eyes back and forth. He begged for the privilege of playing with them, and his eyes became caught on a twig. So the chickadees took some pitch and made him another pair—that is why his eyes are so yellow.

3—Coyote saw the beavers gambling and insisted upon joining their game. They made him put up his beautiful skin, as they did; and, when he lost it, they gave him the rough coat he now has.

Santo Blanco mentioned these last two without prompting of any kind, and said all the old Seris used to sing these songs. They had forgotten them now, but there are others which have taken their places. Here is one of the old ones:

Old Coyote Song

The coyote is happy in the moonlight.
He sings a song to the moon—
While he dances.
And he jumps far away—
While he dances.

But even a little bird
Can jump farther than coyote
When he dances in the moonlight.
If he jumps like the bird
He goes only half as far.

This song probably refers to the chickadees and to the loss of his eyes. Another one is about the loss of his fur:

Coyote Song

One coyote found another one dancing
Very prettily in a circle of *carrizos*
And, while he danced,
He had his paws over his eyes.

So the other coyote
Set fire to the *carrizos*
But coyote kept on dancing,
Because his paws were over his eyes
And he could not see the fire.
So all his fur got scorched brown.

As in all coyote stories the coyote is represented as being crazy to get married, and in the Coyote Dance of the Sahuaro Ceremony he sings this song all the time:

I want to get married
I want to get married—
So he married a *pitahaya* woman.

With the Seris, as with most Western Indians, the coyote is made the butt of many clownish jokes. This song describes his misfortunes. It is sung for the Coyote Dance:

Coyote Dance Song

When the coyote is very hungry
He sings his song—
With his nose on the ground
Running round and round.

When he has sung his song
He is no longer hungry.
When coyote has eaten he is very happy
And he dances
Because he is happy.

When coyote is hungry
He hunts the meat of the jack rabbit.
He will not eat any other kind of meat.
Now he dances—
Because he has eaten the rabbit.

When coyote is hungry
He wanders along the beach
Looking for a dead sea turtle.
He wanders far but he finds no *cahuama*.

The coyote digs the crab
Out of his hole in the sand.

Crab seizes coyote by the nose.
The coyote tries to shake him off
But the crab holds on tight
And coyote cannot shake him off.

The coyote finds a sea spider
On the edge of the water, and bites him.
The octopus winds his arms around coyote's head
And coyote cannot get away.

So he leaves the beach
And runs through the monte
Where the sunshine is hot.
The sun kills Ubari
And he falls to the ground
Where the coyote eats him.

The coyote sings to the gopher-snake
But culebra does not stop.
He runs away rapidly
And coyote cannot catch him.
So he just sings to him.

Santo Blanco was going strong and we let him alone, until he gave us his Happy Song. First he leaned forward, smiling, as he remembered its beginning; then he tapped out the time, as gay and spritely as a jig, while in his soft melodious voice he sang it through to the end. It was hard to believe he was a boat-robbing barbarian, he seemed so much like a scholar and a gentleman. He seemed so much like ourselves—and we let him have his own way.

HAPPY SONG

I sing to all living things with roots.
While I sing, the flowers of all the trees
Are falling, beautifully.
All the petals have fallen
But there is no fruit yet.

Now the mesquite trees are covered with beans
But the pods do not fall yet.
The *pitahayas* are covered with cactus-pears.
The birds with their beaks peck open the fruit.
They are happy.

The fruit of the *pitahaya* is ripe.
The doves say: "I want to eat it."
With his beak he pulls out the fruit.
The *sahueso* has no fruit. It falls to the ground.
Its roots stand up. It is no good.

The time comes when the grass is green
The Lagoon dries up—all the grasses die.
One half of the ironwood is dry,
One half of the ironwood is green,
But it does not fall to the ground.

The *torote* tree is green
And I will make four baskets from its sticks.
From the swamp-willow I will make
A big basket, like an olla.

I have finished my basket.
Eight days it took me to make one half.

Six days more it took to finish it,
With a small mouth.
Now I have finished my basket I am happy.

Santo Blanco smiled again when I told him this
was good; that it was like the songs our poets sang—
only often not as well. It was a poem to Nature, to the
Great God we all sing to. The God who lives everywhere, in everything. Yes, he said, the Seris sang to
everything—he would give me their song to the rattlesnake.

SONG TO THE VIVORA

I sing this song to the rattlesnake.
I sing it to the Big Mountain.
I have fought with the Papagos
And killed many.

I shout because I am happy.
When I come to my house
All along the trail
I dance.

The Papago sings loud
He shoots many shots from his gun.
He dances sideways,
Like a side-winder rattlesnake.

The clouds sing
Because they have rained much water.
The Bow sings his song. He says:
"I am *muy hombre*—a very brave man.
I am strong like a giant."

I will sing this to the Seri—
He is dead.
I sing to the white-tail deer—
He leaps along as he runs.

I hunt the sea turtle at night
Because then he cannot see me.
He sees only a little
When I catch him.

THE LAGOON SINGS

I paint all pictures
And all colors on my face.
Everybody that passes by
I reflect on my face.

The Rain comes.
The River runs high
It overflows its banks.
With it go the snakes.

The rats and the toads.
They are lost in the sea
And the toad cries out: "Caaa-caa!"
When he is out at sea.

The sea runs like a river to the north.
All land is overflowed to the dunes
And fishes die in the sun
As the water goes down.

The whales come to the shore,
Some pinto and some black.

So many they are
Like sardines.

The sea turtle cannot dive
In the muddy water;
He can only swim down a little way.
He swims with his head still out.

Ramona lives alone.

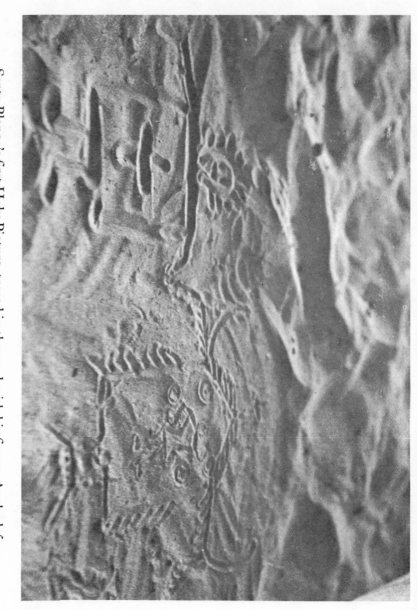

Santo Blanco's first Holy Picture, traced in the sand with his finger. At the left is Father Sky, with rays about his head like the sun and a cross to indicate he is holy. Mother Earth is the central figure to the right, surrounded with four circles for the Sun, Moon, North Star and Morning Star.

(Photograph by Dane Coolidge)

CHAPTER XX

Face Paintings

WHEN I gave Santo Blanco his peso and a half for the many songs he had sung, I knew it was not enough. But poets are used to being underpaid and seem to thrive on very little—just enough to keep them alive and happy. Still Santo Blanco could take care of himself—even while he sang he was thinking out a plan to tap my pocket again.

Buro Alazan, on the last day he had talked, had made some pictures of face paintings, explaining them in his ignorant way, and Santo Blanco had seen the crude drawings. They were done in ink with my fountain pen, but with the names of the colors written in, and Santo Blanco had decided to do them better. So he begged a sheaf of smooth, white paper and took it home.

I had been surprised at the bold strength displayed in Buro's last picture—a shark with its high fin sticking up as it cleft its way through the sea. For a savage —which he undoubtedly was—and for a man using pen and paper for the first time it was certainly a work of art. There were no waste lines, the proportions were good, and for that reason I had kept the sketches. But Santo Blanco, when he returned the next morning, had his face paintings done in *color*—and he knew what every one of them meant.

Here was a new demonstration by this versatile little man that he had an artist's soul, but his hands had been so dirty he had spoiled the effect by numerous thumb-marks and smooches. Nevertheless, I gave him twenty centavos apiece for them and he went into an exposition of Face Paintings which made Buro Alazan look like a fool. Buro's explanations had been as follows:

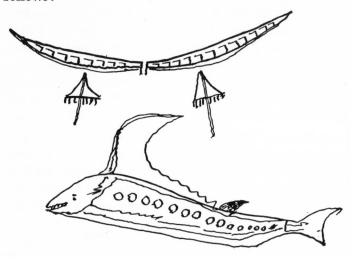

Our first Seri drawing. Buro Alazan pictures the Face Painting which the women put on the faces of their men when they were going out to war. An ancestor of theirs, a great warrior, had told them to do this and they would feel neither pain nor cold.

As an afterthought he made a picture of a Big Shark.

Drawing by Buro Alazan.

"This painting is put on so their faces will be cool. When a girl wants to attract a sweetheart she paints her face pretty. When the man sees these paintings he knows she wants a man. This painting is for girls— just something pretty. It does not represent anything. They leave it on a day or two, then put on another with different colors."

But Santo Blanco was a medicine man, full of exact
information, trained to remember the lore of his people—and to him every face painting had a meaning.
The pictures he brought me had been made by his
own folks—his wife, Loreta Lupe; his slender daughter, Lupe; Candelaria and little Lolita and Lupita.
There were also designs by Margarita, Maria Luisa
and Ramona, all done with great precision and taste.

Each girl had her own little toilette case, containing lumps of blue, red, yellow and black paint, with a
clamshell for mixing colors. Her brush was the chewed
end of a mesquite twig and they used up all the paper
their father had. Old Manuel Encinas had begged a
single sheet and covered it with pictures of the gods—
the Devil of Sickness and the Good Angel with a
Cross, who drove the Evil One away. Such an out-
pouring of primitive design was more than I had expected, but I bought them, every one.

Then I spread them out and made Santo Blanco
name them, with an explanation of every spot and
line. But when I demanded the ages of his seven
daughters I discovered my medicine man's weak spot.
He could not count. Not only that—he seemed to have
no sense of numbers. He could not even guess their
ages. When he told me that the beautiful Lupe, who
had a young Seri waiting to marry her, was only four
years old, I knew that something was wrong. But even
the youngest, who might have been four, displayed a
real feeling for drawing. Face painting was their
highest, their only means of aesthetic expression; and
now, for the first time, they had sheets of white paper
instead of their faces to paint on.

At twenty centavos a picture it came to five or six
pesos; and, when I went to the village to photograph

them, the Seri maidens collected more pay. They were all smiles now, though they shrank from the great eye of the camera, and at last we knew that the women

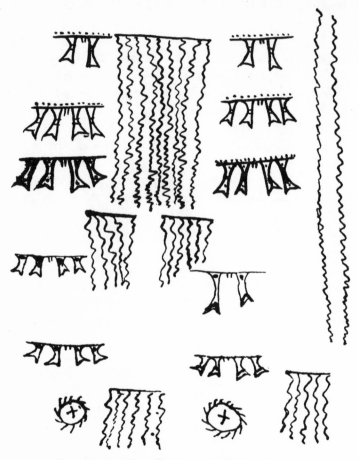

Designs for Face Painting, by Lupe Blanco.

Down the middle, octopus legs.
Down left side, flowers and beans.
Down right side, sea snakes.
At the bottom, moon and sun, with crosses.

had become our friends. From the first they had declined to sit by the interpreter and dictate what they knew; but with white men all Indian women are shy.

It made Santo Blanco feel very important to be the dispenser of so much largess; and back in our tent he spent most of the day explaining the meaning of their paintings.

The Turtle, Coyote, Cactus Pear and Pelican paintings are the most important, as they represent the four great families of the past. In the old days, all who belonged to these four divisions or clans painted the insignia on their faces. The Cactus Pear and Coyote clans are closely related, and their members live on the mainland. The Turtle and Pelican clans are related, and their members live on the Island. In those days, only the Cactus Pears could marry the Turtles. Only the Pelicans could marry the Coyotes. Now there are so few Seris left that the four great divisions are ignored. Men and women can marry anybody except their brothers and sisters and close relatives. Years ago the Seris did not eat the flesh of the Pelican, *Cahuama*, Coyote and *Pitahaya*. Now they do—all except the Coyote. They do not like the Coyote—he is not considered as food.

It was the Coyote who taught the Seris to eat cactus-pears. A woman was watching him, where a *pitahaya* hung close to the ground, and she saw him pick the fruit, brush the needles off in the sand, and eat it. So the woman did the same and found it was very good.

In the Birthday Fiesta the insignia of the Buro Deer, Sea Turtle, Jack Rabbit and Pelican each was painted on the face of some man who wore it during the feast. A fifth man had the picture of a Balsa Canoe painted across his face. He was called the Older One, and ruled the feast. They danced and sang to these four animals, and to all the animals and fishes.

When the month of the birth of a first-born child comes around the following year, this ceremony is carried out—but only once. The months are not

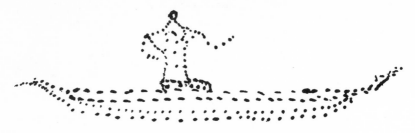

Balsa face painting. Put right across the face.
Drawing by Santo Blanco.

counted in the Yori way. The Seri year begins when the Cactus Pears get ripe—from the middle to the end of May. The composition of the paints is as follows:

The yellow is an iron ocher.

The red is an iron oxide, from the Island of San Estevan. It comes in round, hard balls—very heavy.

The white is gypsum.

Common blue is made by grinding unburned white gypsum in a very little water. Then boil the root of the ah-mahk' bush in water and down to a paste. Mix in a shell with ground gypsum and allow to evaporate until it becomes like a rock. When the artist wants some color he rubs a little down in water, the same as India ink. They also make blue by grinding up a blue stone, found on Tiburon Island.

The pictures used only for ornamentation are called Pretty Face, and each girl designs her own, some con-

The weave of a basket.

Ironwood roots.

The crosses indicate how long the painting will stay on. At the right a four-day painting.

Left, culebra snake painting—along the top and down both sides. Right, ironwood seeds in white on top, with crosses in **blue.**

Left, ironwood seeds in black. Pods below in white. Below them throwing sticks. Right, another basket pattern.

PRETTY FACE PAINTINGS BY MARGARITA BLANCO.

ventionalized and others copied from Nature. They
are mostly in blue and white; though yellow, red and
black are also used. Some of the prettiest are named
after flowers, such as mesquite flowers and ironwood
flowers, a wind-blown maguey flower, and other pretty
fancies. There are basket patterns and ironwood roots,
seeds and pods; sardines in blue and red, curly octopus-
legs in blue, culebra snakes in black with yellow spots;
a galaxy of birds—pelicans, hawks, frigate-birds, and
the little red flycatcher of the monte.

In these drawings they have given their fancy full
flight and, to indicate how long the paintings will be
left on, small crosses are put into the design. There are
two-day paintings and four-day paintings, pictures of
the Sun and Moon, with a cross in the middle and a
whirl of rays all around. I Paint My House On My
Face is one of the most striking, but the houses are
not the modern huts—they are half-circles of woven
strands sheltering the figure of a woman, who stands
with outstretched hands by her fire.

It is the art of women whose only canvas is their
own faces, whose only mirror is a shell of clear water,
reflecting the desert light. But art it is, and the Seri
women were very happy to have their pictures appreciated. They came running to our tent to demand
more and more paper as they remembered long-for-
gotten designs, and we dispensed it with a prodigal
hand; but Santo Blanco, in making the distribution,
took care that his family got the most of it.

This was going to be a gold mine for his eight
daughters, all but one of whom were big enough to
paint; and, since their pictures were better than those
of the other women, we were glad to let them have
all they wanted. Santo Blanco himself went in for

something more ambitious—no less than pictures of the gods.

But at first, to try me out, he leaned over and with his finger traced a picture in the sand. It could have meant much or little, but I recognized it at once as Father Sky and Mother Earth, who have been pictured with a wealth of symbolism in the famous Painting of the Navajos. And, rather than see it destroyed, I held everything until I had photographed it.

At this sign that I appreciated its value, Santo Blanco begged a sheaf of white paper and, when he returned in the morning, he brought with him many pictures of the gods. They were copied, or remembered, from the walls of the Holy Cave on Tiburon and several have been used to illustrate this book— but he never did his first one again.

The Mother Earth and Father Sky is of Asiatic origin, being found in the art and literature of India, China and Japan. But how it came among the Seris and the Navajos is a question difficult to answer. These two tribes have no knowledge of each other, and there is no apparent similarity in their languages, so far as we could ascertain by a comparison of very limited vocabularies. But the picture indicates that at some time in the past, the Seris have come in contact with Asiatic influences.

The fact that they use the Greek Cross, instead of the Latin or crucifixion Cross, would seem to indicate that their religious pictures have not been greatly influenced by the Catholic priests who visited them— although two of these visitors, Ahnt ah zu'-mah and Ahnt ah koh'-mah, had yellow hair and blue eyes and were clad in priestly robes, and one of them has been deified. The rules for living laid down by these two

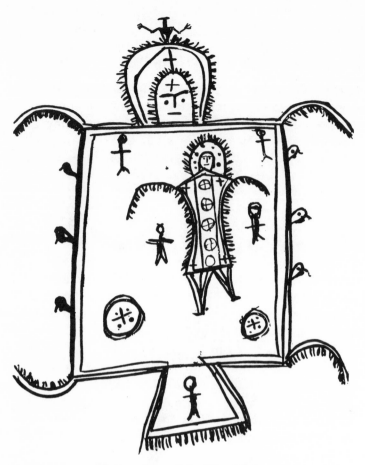

Flying Around In The Night.

This is a copy of the picture on the wall of the Holy Cave, on Tiburon. He rules the earth in the hot weather and the Seri men make offerings of cactus fruit to him. The god is in the middle of the picture marked with four crosses in circles to show that he is holy. The circle without a cross is a sign of sickness. The seven spots around his head are a holy flower, which is black in the daytime and red at night, like a star. The branches are his wings—he is flying—and the halo above his head is feathers.

On four sides of him are little figures, which fly about with him, and a fifth is in his tail. In the lower corners are, the left, the Moon; right, the Sun. The six heads on the outside represent the guardians of the cave and on the top of the picture is his son Ahn tee up—Wants A Flower.

Drawing by Santo Blanco.

men were such as a priest might suggest, and the records of other Mexican tribes tell of similar golden-haired Yoris who taught the people how to live. They

Ahn tee up. Wants A Flower.

Son of Flying Around In The Night. A very good god, but a man-god as shown by his ears and the holes in his palms. He lives in the middle of Tiburon Island and comes out at night to make the flowers grow.

Drawing by Santo Blanco.

were possibly European missionaries, although all of them are reported as coming from the west. The Gulf of California forms a huge pocket on the West Coast of North America—a pocket which has caught and brought to Tiburon the sea-wanderers of the centuries.

But the deities of the Seri religion are more like those of the Greeks—or the ancient world from which the Greeks derived their gods. They have the same Mother Earth and Father Sky. In place of Zeus they have Ahnt ahs' po-mee'-kay—He Who Rules Earth And Sky. Ahnt Kai', like Juno, is the guardian of women and children; and, like the Asiatic Kwan Yin, she is the Goddess of Mercy, to whom the women pray. But it is her little daughter, Ahnt ahs pok', to whom the children pray; and the Greeks had no equivalent for I Am Very Wise. Zeus married his sister, Juno, just as the son and daughter of First Man and First Woman married, and there are other evidences that the religion of the Seris is not that of ignorant savages but is related to other primitives of Europe, Asia and the great outside world.

Lupe Blanco, her face decorated with the delicate flower-picture which indicates that she is willing.

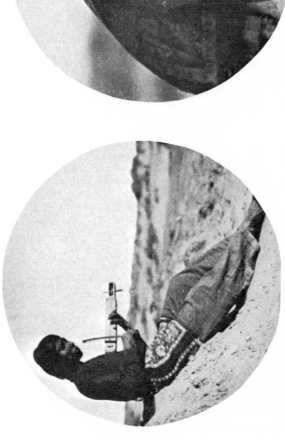

The lover of the beautiful Lupe, playing on his one-string violin.

Santo Blanco, playing the musical bow. By pressing it down on the baskets he makes the string slack or tight, tapping out the music with a stick.

(Photograph by Dane Coolidge)

CHAPTER XXI

Music—and War

THE suitor of the beautiful Lupe was Francisco
Molino, who had accompanied Santo Blanco at
the Fish Dance on his one-string violin. He was a
handsome young savage and was serving a term of
slavery to win her for his wife—a sure sign he loved
her dearly, for Santo Blanco's wife was a shrew. With
three other old women, who looked enough like her to
be sisters, she led a mass-scolding before the house of
the Chiefs every time their actions did not please her.

As the mother of Ramona, she was the center of the
fight over whether a man could have two wives; and
no doubt poor Santo Blanco was leading a dog's life
as she scolded about the matter to him. But Francisco
Molino was suffering more than he; for, as Lupe's
suitor, he had not only to work for her mother but
literally to sleep with the dogs.

All the rest of the Blanco family slept inside the
brush house, with their feet in a circle to the fire.
Francisco coiled up outside the door, with only mongrel dogs for company. But that did not keep him from
singing Seri love songs to the charming but shy Guadalupe—hence the box-shaped fiddle with one string.
Imagine my surprise when he came the following
morning and offered to sell it for one peso!

That seemed to be the standard price for anything
worth more than twenty centavos, but I protested that
he ought not to sell it. Upon what would he play when
he wanted to sing to Guadalupe? He simply stood

dumb until I tired of kidding him and handed him over his peso. It was a shame to deprive him of his fiddle, which was apparently his sole possession, but while I was admiring it Santo Blanco got another idea. A big idea for getting more of my money before I went away and took it with me. That same afternoon he returned with four more instruments—and stripped to the waist to show me how they were played.

First the Musical Bow—which he placed, string up, over the bottoms of two baskets, while he tapped the string with a stick. By pressing the bow down with the other hand he made the string tight or slack and could play a regular tune. So I bought it—and paid him a peso extra for letting me take his picture.

The greedy Chico, in order to trim the tourists, had fixed an arbitrary price of eight pesos for anyone photographing a naked Seri. And, since all wanted them stripped to the waist, he made a very good thing of it. But not with me—I refused to pay—so Santo Blanco reduced his price. He knew, if the Chief did not, what a tourist would or would not pay, and one peso was my limit.

Then he brought out his musical stick, putting one end on the bottom of an upturned basket while he raked its notched side with a stick. It made a noise like nothing so much as a chorus of frogs croaking—which is what the Hopi Indians use it for in their Return of the Katchina Dance, put on to make it rain. Very good! I gave him a peso for that, and he let me take the picture for nothing. With his pelican-skin skirt and the crown of Ahnt ah zu'-mah, which he had made especially for this purpose!

I gave him another peso for that, when the orgy of photographing was over, and he let me take his picture for nothing while he shook his tin-can rattles. These were called *Eh-hez'*—rattle—and were used in place of the gourds which had formerly served that purpose. They were simply two condensed-milk cans thrust through with sticks for handles, and with corn grains to rattle inside. They made a musical note, as clear and chinging as sleigh bells, and were much better than the old-fashioned *guapes*, or gourds, so common in the Southwest.

Though they made very good music and had been used when he sang the Fish Dance, I beat him down to fifty centavos, so that he would not think I was too easy. Then he brought out his sublimated Jew's Harp —a hollow reed, with one string stretched the length of it on a peg and with holes along the side like a flute. He strummed the string while he blew into the tube, and a cheery note came forth. It was called Hurry Play, and was used purely as an instrument of joy. When a child was born—or at a wedding—and when they were happy from mezcal "or any other kind of liquor."

This exhausted his store of musical instruments, and I bought it to round out my collection. A very good showing for a bunch of savages, who might have to pick up and move any time. Already I had the fiddle! *Enzl* it was called—A Crying—and I asked if they had any more stringed instruments. Yes, they had a one-string viol, descended from their old Seri Harp —which had been made of hollow maguey stalks and eleven gut-strings. It stood tall as a man and was played with the thumb, a change of tone being made by pressing down with the foot on the board at the bottom, thus tightening or loosening the string. Quite an ingenious stunt for an itinerant artist—to reduce his strings from eleven to one. This viol was called One String.

But this was not all. The observant Seris had discovered that, if you drive a spear into a sea turtle and kill him quickly, you can *tum, tum* on the spear handle and make a pleasant note. This is merely a dead *cahuama* and it is not used in any ceremony but just as a musical instrument. It is called Quickly Killed Sea Turtle.

Yet another instrument is made out of the land tortoise, called Hollow Shell of a Tortoise. The tortoise is killed by turning him on his back in the sun. Then the insides are taken out, the shell is dried, and small stones are put into it. It is held in the two hands, one covering each of the openings, and shaken like a rattle.

We must include in the list the half-section of a sea-turtle shell, which is placed over a shallow hole for a sounding board when a dancer is beating time for the songs. It gives the effect of a drum and can be heard for a mile or more.

The tenth and last instrument is the Conch Shell— Shell Found by the Sea. The tip of the small end is cut off and the conch is blown to summon home the children, when they are out hunting cactus-pears in the hot season. It is also used as a signal to announce people coming to a feast; and in war, when they have been scattered in a retreat, to call the people together again.

Here are ten musical instruments, all made without the use of metal by a tribe still living in the Stone Age. It seems to indicate that, at some time in the past, they were possessed of a higher culture—and to account for the beauty of their songs and the intricate rhythms of their dance steps. Santo Blanco was greatly pleased when complimented on his performance and settled down to earn a peso and half more by telling a few more stories of implements and methods used in war.

A blue fire is used as a war signal, to summon the men when they are going to war. It is made by burning dry wood which has been soaked in salt water along the beach, and they make a very large fire. Many men encircle it, dancing slowly; while on the outside, with their backs to the flame, four big men keep watch. The fire blinds their enemies, while it reveals their approach to the watchers. If there are a hundred men there is one fire—four hundred men, four fires. But Santo Blanco has never seen over two hundred men in battle.

The use of guns—*pitardos*—was originally learned from the Mexican soldiers, who fought against the Seris for many years with cap-and-ball muskets. Later, the Seris learned to imitate these guns by making them from a section of water-pipe with one end plugged for the breach and a small hole left in the side of it. Into this they inserted the head of an old-fashioned snap-match, which was struck with a stone to ignite the powder in the barrel. A stick, like the tail of a rocket, was bound to the breach for a stock.

Whenever the Seris killed a Yori they would take, besides his gun, his powder pouch and bullets and use them to load their *pitardos*, which they call I Have A Gun. In the old days the Seris used to kill Mexicans with these guns.

Before the ranchers and soldiers came with their guns, the Seris would fight with the bow and arrow, and with a fighting stone—ahst. Points were left on the rock to puncture the skull. The rock was not thrown but used like the fist, to strike with, and it would break a skull, an arm or a leg. They wore armor down to the knees, made from sea-lion skin. On top of this armor they had flat stones, tied over their chest, and sometimes one on each side of the head. The only place an arrow could strike them was in the upper face. The helmet was separate, with long plumes made of crow feathers—two long ones underneath and then two, shorter and shorter. The plumes did not stand up, but went over behind.

In the early days they fought with the ahst alone— no other arms. Then with knives made of bone. Then they began to learn to use the bow and arrow—not from other Indians but from their old people.

When the Seris went to war every man carried two ollas; one full of meal ground from the eelgrass seed, and one full of water. They also carried a large clam-shell to mix it in, like atole. Whenever they went out to fight they left the women behind on the Island. In the early days they had bows and arrows for hunting but did not take them with them to war. Under each arm the warriors carried a sea-lion skin full of round stones off the beach, as big as a man's fist. When they met the Papagos, the Papagos let fly all their arrows. Then the Seris charged and, on the silty desert, the Papagos were helpless, having no rocks. They could only strike with their bows. When the Seri got close to an enemy, he threw a stone at his chest or head. If it hit him it would either kill him or knock him down; and, if not dead, they would kill him with a blow. In one battle, two hundred Papagos were killed and not a single Seri. When the warriors came back they had an eight-day fiesta, in which all the children joined.

When they went to war with other tribes they would have a dance first; and after the fight, if victorious, they would have a big fiesta, in which all the men and women joined, dancing in a big circle. The children were all put off to one side, where they could look on. After the battle, the old men who had not gone out would sit inside the circle, even if they were so old they were blind. They would sit in the circle and sing.

When they came back from a battle which they had lost, there would be no fiesta. They were very sad then, and the women would cry, not loud, for one day. Then they would paint their faces black for four days.

When they killed enemies they tried to get them where they could take a piece of their scalp. The scalps were taken up the middle of the head from the back of the neck to the forehead. The scalp was hung up on a long pole in the brush, and it had to be tied firmly to this stick so it could not fall down. As long as it stayed tied on the stick it was good luck to them but if it fell down it was bad luck and they would not go to war for a long time afterward, because they knew many Seris would be killed. If they wanted to go to war, they went first to see that all the scalps were hanging on their poles—they had a separate pole for each one. The scalp that was farthest from the houses was the one that counted, and if it was down they would not fight until some other occasion. If the scalps were still there it was a good sign and the preparations went on.

They had an old medicine man who would sing before they went to war. They did not sing over the scalp—they sang to the old Seris, the spirits of the old warriors. The old man sang so the Seris would win. When they came back all the warriors would sing with him, but on starting out only the old medicine man would sing. He did not go to war.

They had two war captains. One went ahead, and the men would follow. The other stayed behind and he would follow the men. The man that stayed behind was the Big Chief, who told them what to do, the same as the soldiers in Hermosillo.

The Seris sometimes fought at night, the same as in the day. Whether killed in the daytime or at night they went to heaven; but, if a Seri was stabbed with a knife and the blood ran out of him, he could not go to heaven. He would be buried with a little dirt over him and his spirit would wander around at night just like the wind, without any direction. Because when a man's blood came out of him he could not talk to God.

CHAPTER XXII

The Three Hundred and Fifty Songs

IN THE four ceremonies where a man dances on a plank the medicine man sings three hundred and fifty songs—different songs every night. The dancer knows the songs also, and when he starts a shuffle it helps the singer remember the words, because the words and the beating of his feet have the same rhythm. Every song has a dance step of its own. These three hundred and fifty songs are sung at the Fish Dance, the *Pitahaya* Feast, the Pelican Feast, and at any Marriage Feast in the *pitahaya* season.

As a preliminary to any song sequence where they are going to dance on a plank, the following song is sung:

> Come on and dance!
> Come on and dance!
> Hurry up!

Each of the night chants is ended with the Old Wise Woman's song to Tiburon, much as we sing "America."

THE ISLAND SINGS:

> Watch me dance!
> I am heavy, but I can dance!
> See the edge of my skirt
> Wave back and forth.
>
> It is the waves of the sea
> On my beach.

In this song the Island is compared to a woman dancer, wearing long skirts; and the conception of the white waves being the fringe of her dress is certainly far from a primitive one. Incidentally, it dates back to a time when women wore skirts which swept the ground—whereas the modern Seri women wore nothing but pelican skins until they procured *manta* from the Mexicans.

Santo Blanco was pleased to have this song praised and said it had been composed by the Old Wise Woman who had landed on their Island long ago. When she came the Seris knew nothing, and she taught them many chants and ceremonies, including the Women's Fiesta. First she taught her husband, who knew nothing till she told him. Then she taught the others everything they knew in those days.

She never died, although the Seris do not see her now. She lives in the middle of the Island and flies around at night, watching over them. For this reason she is called Flying Around In The Sky. Her songs were passed on among the Seris, and Santo Blanco learned them from an old white-haired medicine man who lived on the north end of the Island. He continued with fourteen of them, ending with the Song of the Whale, which is given on page ——.

SONG OF THE MULLET:

With my spear in my hand
I sing to the fish.
Many come leaping from the water.
With my spear I kill them.
Many children are hungry at home,
I know they are waiting for me

Even if I have only one fish.
When I spear one, all the rest
Disappear into the deep water.
With my one fish I go home.

When the fisherman gets home, the entrails and the head of the fish are roasted on the coals. They cook quickly, and the children eat them while the rest of the fish is being cooked.

The Mullet That Was Speared:

The sea is calm
But, close to my boat,
A little breeze stirs the water.
It is one mullet
That stirs the water.
I spear him but he does not die.

When the man speared this mullet the fish turned red, like blood. All his children were red like blood. All other mullets are silvery and dark.

After the female turtle has laid her eggs, the male comes and seeks out her nest on the beach. The baby loggerhead has a very small body, with a large head and long flippers. The mother guards the nest until her little ones hatch out, sometimes as many as two hundred.

The Giant Turtle Sings:

I come from the deep water,
To find the eggs
Which the female has laid.
On the sand dunes I find her nest

And uncover many eggs.
They will hatch next month
So I cover them up again.

THE PADDLE SINGS:

The wind is strong and I work hard
But I cannot bring the balsa to shore.
I am tired and go to sleep
Because I cannot bring the boat to my house.

When I awaken I am close to the shore.
When I awaken I am strong
I am no longer tired.
With four turtles in my balsa
I paddle to the shore.

When the paddle gets tired, he takes a little piece of
meat from the neck of a turtle and eats it raw. Then
he goes to sleep and when he wakes up he is strong.

THE SONG OF THE PANGO CANOE:

My pango is fast.
It has traveled the small seas
And the big ones.
It has traveled by the shore
And over the deep water
Where there is no land.
With me it goes so fast
It leaves the sailboats behind,
So I only have to use the paddle.

This song was composed by an old man who is now
dead. When he was alive he had a modern canoe, or

pango, not a balsa. Among the Ancients the canoe was not known—not until the Second Seris came. That was about two thousand years ago—then they had boats. The First Seris were "five thousand" years ago.

A BALSA SONG:

The air was cold.
A man sat on his balsa.
He had paddled long
And was very tired.

The tide ran swiftly
Away from his home.
He was tired and cold
And could paddle no more.

He fell asleep
With his paddle across his knee.
When he awoke
His balsa had brought him home.

His wife came out
With all her neighbors.
They took his hand
And led him to his house.

Each one said:
"You will not die,
Though you are so cold and tired
You will not die."

And the balsa sang to him:
"You will not die.
You were cold and tired
But I brought you home."

The Sea Lion Song:

The little *lobo* was born pure white,
Although his mother was black.
For two days he lay on the beach—
For twenty days he ate no fish.

When his mother brought little fish
And laid them around him
He would not eat them.
But when she brought him a sea snake
He ate it.

The Seris never kill a sea lion, out of pity. They call it *"pobrecito"*—poor little one—and pull its little flippers, shaped like hands; but it never bites them. The sea snakes which it eats are eels.

The Sea Otter is called *Perro del Mar*—Dog of the Sea—and they are very fierce. They come ashore and kill the Seris' dogs.

The Sea Otter Song:

The Sea Otter is very brave.
He has long hair
And the Seri arrows
Will not go through him.

The seal-hunter is afraid
To go into the water,
Because the otter is near
And will kill him.

The Sea Otter has long, soft hair
That parts down the middle of his back.

And over the back of his neck
His hair is longest.

The Seris are afraid
And will not look at him.
His whiskers are very long—
White, black and red.

They fear his whiskers most
Because they make him look so ugly,
And stick out like arrows
When he is mad.

A song sung by an old man when the Seris first saw
cattle. This bull was snow-white all over, except his
eyes, which were very red.

A Song of the Bull:

The bull is very fierce.
He paws the ground,
Throwing dirt on his back.
He makes a loud noise,
So the earth trembles.

The warrior stands before him.
He cannot escape.
When the bull runs after him
The warrior cannot flee,
Because he is afraid.

The bull's horn goes through him
And sticks out his back.
This was no living creature—
He was a spirit that feared nothing.

He walked out at night
The same as he walked by day.

FAST HORSE:

I am playing with my companions.
We run.
I run so fast I leave him behind,
And he runs staggering.
The blood flows from his mouth.

SONG OF A YOUNG MAN:

I run a race
With a man who is very fleet.
With us runs an old man
Who is fleet-footed,
And an old woman
Who is very fast.

My young companion
Runs evenly with me
And we reach the line together.
The old man is close behind.
He is winning when the woman shouts
And he staggers and falls dead.
The old woman crosses the line.

The Ancient Seris told of an enormous deer that
lived on Tiburon Island. He was bigger than any
horse. His horns were broad, like your hands, and
spread out. (Perhaps reminiscent of a moose seen in
the north.) He lived up in the mountains and never
came down into the valleys.

SONG OF THE GIANT DEER:

Four men go out to kill the big deer.
When he comes they are so frightened they die
And the deer eats them, making a loud noise.
He is more fierce than the dog-eating sea otter.
We will not hunt him any more.

THE GIANT DEER SINGS FOR RAIN:

"I have no water and am very thirsty.
The hills are dry—I will call for rain."
A small cloud came and answered him;
Then many clouds, and much rain fell.

For four days it fell
And no Seri could eat,
Nor any of the animals
Because it rained so much.
The Big Deer himself could not eat.

All the animals were hungry
And the Seris were hungry,
And they sang for four days
Begging the clouds to go away.

Then the clouds went far off
And thunder fell only on the mountain.
For four months there was no rain or clouds
So they asked the deer to sing again.

When he sang—far off the thunder blasted.
Then a breeze came towards them that was cool.
A little shower drifted across the sky.
It just dripped. Then a black cloud came
And for four days it gave them water.

CHAPTER XXIII

Mourning Ceremony and the Man's Song

THE Seris are forgetting their many songs and ceremonies. Only the old men and women remember them now, and they are passing away. Besides the four great Four-night Chants, which they still sing, there is the Man's Ceremony and the Women's Fiesta, but it is a long time since these dances have been held. Santo Blanco has never seen the Man's Dance; and, since the Seris began living around the white men's places and getting their food from them, the Woman's Dance has never been given.

There is also a Mourning Ceremony, where they mourn four nights over any calamity. This ceremony is not sung every year but, when they feel sad over the thoughts of their dead, they have a Mourning. The Chief orders it. When women and children were killed by the soldiers on the beach, and when they had other deaths, they had a dance in which—one man at a time, holding an emblem of what killed the person above their heads—they sang to the spirits of the dead.

When Juan Tomas's first wife was killed by the soldiers he danced with a machete held aloft. The widowers of other women followed, each singing for his wife.

MOURNING CEREMONY SONG:
(Sung by the spirit of the woman)
I am happy.
I have left here.

224

It was a sword that killed me.
But I am happy
Because I am dead.

If the person was killed by lightning, a crooked
stick was held up; if by an animal, a figure like an
animal; and in place of the word "sword" the name of
another cause is given. Where a warrior had been
killed in battle, they held above their heads a bow and
quiver full of arrows while they sang.

WARRIOR'S DEATH SONG:

I am happy.
This is the arrow that killed me.
The arrow is happy
Because it took me away from here.

Twenty years ago all the men danced in the Mourning Ceremony. On one side, some distance away, sat
eight old women, their faces painted black. The other
women sat in a big circle, but not near the eight
mourners. The men danced in a circle, holding the
emblem of what had killed the person above their
heads, each man representing the spirit of one who
had died or been killed.

As the mourners cry, the tears run down their
cheeks. The women are careful not to touch these tear
marks. Not for two months do they wash them off,
which makes their faces look like the cracked bottom
of a dry lake. At the end of the two months they wash
their faces in fresh water and paint them white. Then
they say: "Now I am happy."

During this ceremony, and after it, they must not
look back nor step backward; they must not look to

the side nor step aside. They must look ahead and move ahead. If they look or step backward or to either side, blindness will come upon them.

There is a four-day mourning period, when all the men are sad when a man dies. When a woman dies all the women are sad and wail for eight days. If a woman's husband dies, she mourns and cries at intervals for thirty days and paints her face black. She paints it white then, until all sadness is gone. While she is mourning she wears no necklaces or ornaments. When she is ready to marry again—eight, fifteen or many months later—she paints her face very beautifully in all the colors she can get and every day she paints it afresh, so it looks nice. She hangs many necklaces around her neck until the longer ones reach to her waist. When the marriageable men see this they say:

"Now she is happy." And someone marries her.

The Man's Ceremony is held in May, the Seris' New Year. Four lines of men dance forward and back, surrounded by a square of men who do not dance. Down the middle dances a very old woman, making little jumps back and forth. She sings as she dances. No other women are allowed near.

Each man ties on his head, one on each side, an arrow sticking straight up. Around his waist he wears a pelican skin. The old woman has one arrow sticking up straight. The men carry nothing in their hands— no clothes or personal belongings; all their stuff is put away off in the houses where they live. They dance four nights. It is a man's ceremony, but boys of all ages come and dance.

At the corners of the square four live animals are staked out—the buro deer, the jack rabbit, the moun-

tain sheep and the sea turtle. The sea turtle is caught
when he is left stranded on the beach after a high
tide. Then men dig a pit where it will fill up with
salt water, and keep the *cahuama* there till fiesta time.
The other animals are caught while they are young
and kept staked out at the houses, where they are fed.
In the oldest Man Dance, before Santo Blanco's time,
they had a crab present, because the crab was the first
thing they learned to kill and eat.

SONGS OF THE MAN'S CEREMONY:

(The Old Woman in the center of the square sings
for the men.)

1   The New Year is beginning
     And so I dance.

2   All over the mountains
     I hunt the sheep.
     All through the monte
     I hunt the buro
     And the jack rabbit.
     In the sea
     I hunt the turtle.

3   The sea comes up
     And covers the beach.
     The *cahuama* is left stranded.
     I catch him.

4   I dig a pit
     To hold the turtle.
     It is full of sea water
     And no stick holds him.

5   The deer and the jack rabbit
    And the mountain sheep
    Are tied by the hands.
    They cry.

When a hunter returns from a kill he puts blood on his face. The first person who recognizes the blood and knows what animal it comes from is entitled to the first portion of the meat. The blood of the turtle is dark red, that of the mountain sheep bright red, that of the jack rabbit whitish-red, that of the deer yellowish-red. The four animals at the corners are all alive. They are put there so they can see the dance and know that these are the men who have killed these animals in the past.

The first ones who dance are the men who have killed these different animals. Each one paints his face with the blood of the animal he has killed at some time. The young men see all this, which is to teach them how to kill the animal.

The Old Woman holds an arrow aloft. No blood drips from the arrow point. She points it to the square of outside men, who have never killed any of these animals.

Blood of the Turtle drips from the arrow point, and she points to the men who have killed turtles.

Blood of the Deer drips from the arrow point, and she points to the men who have killed deer.

Blood of the jack rabbit drips from the arrow point, and she points to the men who have killed jack rabbits.

Blood of the mountain sheep drips from the arrow point and she points to the men who have killed mountain sheep.

The animals are all dead now.

The Old Woman sings:

    6   All you who have killed these animals
        Come and dance with me.

    7   Come dance with me.
        From the big mountain
        Comes the Holy One.

She dances with a little figure of this god in her hand, inviting him to come. His spirit comes and sits outside the square. He raises his hands and says:

"Now they have sung to me."

Then he turns away from them with arms outstretched and says,

"I have been here."

He goes back to the Holy Cave.

This Spirit is pure white, and light shines from the ends of his fingers. The woman who lives in the Cave is all black except her face, which is white. When she is alone in the Cave it is black on the inside, like night; but when the Spirit enters it is as bright as day.

There is no mouth to this Cave except when they open it. It is opened by the Spirit making a cross on the face of the rock. When he wants to come out he breathes on the inside and the door opens. Behind the Man's Cave, and deep down in the earth, is the Woman's Cave, all painted in beautiful colors.

After the Spirit has departed the Old Woman sings this song, but she does not dance.

    8   The Cave Sings:

        With his hand the Spirit opens the Cave
        He stands far from the door

And the woman comes to him.
She touches his hands.
He follows her as she turns back
Into the Cave.

9   The Old Woman Sings for the Spirit:

I am in the dark, but I know darkness.
It does not trouble me.
The dark is the same as the light.

10   The Old Woman Sings:

From a ripe mother rattlesnake
I take a handful of little ones.
I hold them in the palm of my hand
And the snake bites cannot hurt me.

She rubs these little rattlesnakes on her breast and
the Father of Rattlesnakes cannot hurt her.
This ends the Man's Ceremony.

CHAPTER XXIV

The Women's Fiesta

IN THE month of May, when all the flowers are in
bloom, the women give their Circle Dance. None
of the men are allowed near—they must sleep and
stay far off. During the four days of the dance, each
woman takes the part of a certain flower, which is
painted on her face afresh every day. While she is
dancing she wears flowers in her hair, interwoven
with a wreath of green leaves.

At sunrise baskets of flowers—all the kinds of
which the fruit is not eaten—are laid in a circle outside the dance-ground. In its center is the singer, an
old man—the only man allowed to look on. Around
him is a small circle of little girls, then a larger circle
of older girls. The third circle is composed of young
married women, and in the outside circle are all the
old women.

At the end of the four days the baskets in the outside ring are turned over, covering the flowers, which
are left there for four days more. Then the women
bathe in the sea and wash off all the paint from their
faces.

The Old Man who sings wears four kinds of cactus-
flowers—*pitahaya, sahuaro, sahuesa* and *cina*, called
old-man cactus on account of its white top. Manuel
Encinas is the Old Man now and standing in the
center of the circles, he sings the following stanzas.
Each time he has sung ten a woman tells him. They
are given in the exact order of the sequence.

231

1   The plants are growing.
    They are green now
    But they are all coming into flower.
    Soon will be the New Year
    So let us dance!

2   Now all the grasses are green.
    They have grown each day.
    All the plants have blossoms.

3   With wreaths on our heads
    We will gather *pitahayas*.
    When they are ripe
    The baskets on our heads
    Will be full.

4   *Sung by the quail—in imitation of its call.*

    The *pitahayas* are ripe
    The *pitahayas* are ripe
    The *pitahayas* are ripe.

    People will eat them.
    But I will eat
    Only the flowers
    Of the palo verde.

The Juanico bears flowers when all the others are
barren; it dies down when all the others are green.

5   The San Juanico is dead.
    No blossoms fall from it.
    All other plants
    Drop flowers on the ground.

6   When the year returns
    It will grow again.
    Very small—from the roots.

7   The ironwood is green and growing.
    Only one branch is dead.
    It falls to the ground.

8   Young girls who are lazy
    Do not go out to gather *pitahayas*.

9   The good women go out many days
    Gathering *pitahayas*
    Sahuaros and *sahuesas*.
    Five women have brought in
    Many basketfuls of fruit.

10   The old women say
    The weather is too hot,
    But they are not lazy
    At midday they cannot work.

11   The fruit is not ready to be picked—
    The flower has fallen
    But the fruit is not ripe.

While the dance is going on each girl leaves the circle and dances to her particular plant. When she returns she brings its fruit or flower in her hand.

In this verse the women dance back and forth, shuffling their feet straight ahead or backward while they sing with the Old Man.

12   All the trees and flowers of the plains
    Sing as they dance toward us.

13   The mesquite bean is ripening.
      It is covered with white beans.
      Only a little pink
      Can be seen on the pods.

14   The *palo blanco* sheds its seeds.
      They fall to the ground.
      When the time comes next year
      The little *palo blancos*
      Will spring up from the ground.

15   *The Paloma Dove Sings:*

      I eat my fill of *pitahayas*.
      To my little ones on the nest
      I open my bill and feed them.

When the men go hunting they hang their meat in
a tree for the women to carry home; and drink from
the barrel-cactus.

16   The men go forth to hunt.
      The heat makes them suffer.
      Thirst overpowers them.

17   The woman goes into the brush
      With an olla of water for her man,
      But she misses him as he returns.
      She knows thirst and drinks the water
      As she follows him home.

In the heat of summer the desert tortoise burrows
out caves.

18 *The Little Mountain Sings:*

I am only very small
But under my body
Many turtles dig their homes
And sleep while it is hot.

19 *The Mountain Sheep Sings:*

I live on the high peaks.
The feed is scarce.
I do not go to the plain.

20 *The Giant Ray Sings:*

I have eaten no men.
They say I have,
But only the wood
Of their balsas
Have I eaten.

In ancient times the women knew as much about animals as the men. They knew the names of everything, and taught them to the men. So they sing these songs.

21 *The Cottontail Rabbit Sings:*

The rabbit runs fast,
Behind him is coming the coyote.
He catches him in his mouth.
All his body—skin, meat and guts—
He eats. Then Coyote sings:
"Ai-ai-ai!" (Imitating the coyote.)

22 The sea turtle hears the rush of the canoe.
He knows a spear is coming
And dives deep into the water.

23   A young girl and a young boy
     Meet in the monte.
     He hears her singing.
     He takes her hand,
     And they dance together.
     Four days they dance
     But they are not married.

24   The babies dance around the house
     Like the old ones.
     The older people watch them.

25   *The Little Sting Ray Sings:*

     All along the edge
     Of the water I swim.
     While the sun is hot, I swim.
     When it is cold I go away.

Here the tone of the songs changes abruptly. Those
which follow were probably added by some clownish
singer.

26   I circle myself.
          (he goes around in a small circle)
     Now I seat myself
     And all of you must sing:
     "I circle myself,"
     And dance around in a circle.
          (they sing and dance)

27   *The Old Man Sings:*

     I will teach you a new dance.
     Sing with me what I sing.

28   Dance like me!
      Dance like me!
      I am the road-runner,
      Who does not fly.
          (he lifts his knees high and prances)

29   *The Mocking-bird Sings:*

      Dance like me!
      Dance like me!
          (the Old Man dances mincingly up and
          down in one place like a mocking-bird sing-
          ing)

30   *The Hen Sings This Song.*

      I do not dance
      I do not sing.
      Though you dance
      I will not dance.
      Because I am full of eggs
      I will not sing.

In Seriland there are big caterpillars that eat bugs.

31   *The Caterpillar Sings:*

      I am hungry.
      I come from my hole.
      All the bugs
      Sit around their houses
      And I eat them.

32   *Cameleon', the Lizard, Sings:*

      I sing to the fly:
      "Keep still. Do not dance

And I will eat you
Until I am full,
Then go to sleep on a branch."

When the Seris build a new house the little children
have a party. They eat things and dance, singing this
song with their mother. That is how she teaches them
to sing.

34   *The Buro Deer Sings:*

All night while I feed in the valley
I hear the people singing.
When I am full and go to the hillside
They still are singing.

35   *Buro Sings:*

The wind blows strong.
I cannot hear the man coming
But his body comes to my nose.
I stamp and snort: "*Pwew—pwew—pwew!*"
I run away.

36   *The Baby Buro Sings:*

I wait for my mother
Underneath a bush
While she goes off to feed.
She does not come
So I cry to her:
Whee-hee-hee-hee!
The mother answers:
Moooo-woooo-oo-oo!

37 *The Buck Buro Sings:*

> I am wounded
> On the mountain.
> I cannot go away
> Nor climb the hills.

38 Behind me comes a coyote,
> Following my blood.
> Then five coyotes come.
> They walk around me.
> I cannot get up—
> I know I shall be eaten.

39 *An Old Buck Buro Sings:*

> I walk along slowly
> Because I am old.
> I look for food
> My teeth are gone.
> When I find the ironwood sprout
> I cannot eat it.

40 *The Pelican Sings:*

> The ancient pelican
> Did not eat sardines.
> Now he has learned to dance
> He eats them.

41 The ancient pelican could not fly.
> He caught the sardines
> Only with his beak
> As he sat on the water.
> When he learned to dance
> He taught all the others
> To dance and to fly.

42   *The* Pitahaya *Dove Sings:*

> High on the tip of the *pitahaya*
> I find the ripe fruit.

43   The widow dances
> Among the young girls.
> She is jealous of them.

44   *The Island Sings:*

> Watch me dance!
> I am heavy, but I can dance!
> See the edge of my skirt
> Wave back and forth.
>
> It is the waves of the sea
> On my beach.

This last one, to the Island, is danced every one of the four nights and ends the songs for that night. The Old Man who is singing for the women dances heavily as he impersonates the Island, and gradually sinks down until he is crouched on the ground.

There is another Fiesta—To the Island. The first night they sing one song, all night; the second night, a second song; and so on until there are four.

45   *Song of the Island. First Night.*

> Watch me dance!
> See where my feet go!
> They do not step here
> They do not step there
> They only step in this place
> On my beach.

If the Island steps out of that place it will turn the world over.

46   *Song of the Second Night. The Mirage.*

Watch me dance!
I raise myself above the water!
The wind which blew around me
Blows under me now.
So I do not come down
On my beach.

When there is a mirage, the Island seems to rise and float above the water, as if the wind were blowing under it. Here Santo Blanco paused and fell into deep thought. Then he said:

"There is one verse I do not know. All the trees and plants and bushes know this song, but I have forgotten it."

CHAPTER XXV

The White Whalers

THERE was something strange about this sudden
lapse on the part of Santo Blanco. In nearly a
month of singing his memory had never failed; but
now, with the most beautiful sequence of all, he could
not remember the last verse! Perhaps the spirit of Old
Wise Woman, flying around in the sky, had whispered
a word of warning in his ear. Perhaps this was not a
song to be given in its entirety to one of alien blood.

But we were getting closer to the hearts of these
people—as close as we would ever get—and if he did
not choose to finish this song, no doubt he had good
reasons. He drooped his sad eyes and sat thinking a
long time. Then he tapped his finger to the rhythm of
the dance and began—another song.

47   *The Horse Sings:*

> Watch me dance!
> I am the horse that dances!
> With long bounds I dance
> Back and forth.

It was very good but something was lacking—the
grace and dignity of "The Island Sings," its beauty
and its imagery.

"Did the Old Wise Woman make this song?" I
asked; and Santo Blanco shook his head.

"No," he said. "But she sang other songs."

He smiled hopefully and we let him go on.

48 *The Old Wise Woman Sings:*

I look far away
To where eight houses are.
The men only dance
Though there is no feast.

49 *Phosphorescence:*

The night is calm,
No wind blows.
The sea is lightened like day
With the little lights that come
When the sea is calm
And fishes move in the water.

50 In one month
The boy will marry.
He has a sweetheart
So he will marry.

51 When the *cahuama*
Comes to my house
And has not been killed
He makes sleep come to me.

52 *Song of the Baby Shark:*

Only one day
Have I been born.
Only one night
Have I been born.
Now I can swim—
Now I can eat seaweed.

53 *A Mero Fish Sings:*

> I come to the Lagoon
> But find no fish to eat.
> With my head I bore a hole
> And eat black mud.

Eelgrass was the first food of the Seris. A feast was held every year when the seeds were ripe. This song was sung while the women threshed them out with an ocotillo pole. They wore a crown made of eelgrass. The stalks stood up straight on their heads.

54 *Eelgrass Sings:*

> I am not the waves of the sea,
> Though my branches
> Bend and straighten
> In the wind.

The Seris did not know how to cook the beans of the ironwood before the Wise Woman came. She told them to gather the beans when the pod was sweet, grind it and make cakes, with a little fat. The women sing this song when they are making these cakes.

55 *Old Wise Woman Sings:*

> You do not know
> How to cook ironwood beans.
>
> Eat them this way
> And you will like it.
>
> I grind the seeds
> And bake them with fat.

This is a very old war song that is not sung now. When it was sung, the men still wore the crowns of Ahnt ah zu′-mah.

56 *Song Before a Battle:*

> Let's go and fight!
> We are so brave.
> Let's go and fight!
> Let's go and fight!

Santo Blanco was getting tired—the fount of his inspiration was running dry. He had passed from the dignity of The Island Sings to Fish songs and How To Cook Beans. But he had given of his best—and it was time for us to leave Kino Bay. For two days the wind had been swooping in from the southwest—and, by another sign, we knew it would rain.

Two days before, while others were parting with their treasures, old Manuel Encinas had brought down his rain-maker to sell. It was just a joint of bamboo provided with a plug, and contained nothing but blue sand. When, to beat him down a little on his price, I had professed to doubt its efficacy, he had shaken a little of the sand towards the south—and sung a magic song. Then he had warned me not to shake out any more, and reduced his price to one peso.

I had plugged the holder tight and put it away in my war-bag, but that night the wind began to blow. Perhaps he had spilled too much! Black clouds came scudding across the desert, to gather above Tiburon, and we began to pack our things—a long task. The Indians knew then that we really intended to go, and they came hurrying with more treasures to sell. Santo Blanco parted with the Ahnt ah zu′-mah crown which he had made to wear for his picture, and his wife and daughters went to work on another basket carrier when the old coil they offered was refused. Buro Alazan disposed of his "boy's bow" which would shoot an arrow out of sight, instead of making us a "man's bow" which would shoot through the body of a deer.

The money was flowing like water and Santo Blanco was getting his full share; but the next morning he appeared early, to earn his last *peso y medio*. It was very little in exchange for what he gave, but I had not been satisfied about that last verse, which he had forgotten while singing the Island Song. I knew he could give it, if he would. We were very busy, there was a great deal of packing to be done, and the big tent was slatting in the wind. So I asked him if he had remembered the words. And, if all the trees and plants and bushes knew the words of that beautiful song, why had he not asked them? He thought a while, digging his bare feet into the sand, and looked up with a slow smile.

"I have thought of another song," he said. "About the white giants that came to Tiburon."

"Very well," I said. "I am very busy, but we will stop and write it down."

Every day as we prepared to go, his songs had been getting better and better, and I knew this must be something good. He had been saving it up all the time.

THE WHITE GIANTS

There was a race of white giants who came here long ago. We called them Ahnt'-tay ah hek'-tahm— Came From Afar Men. They had white hair and were so big it took two *fanegas* (bushels) of tobacco to fill their pipes. They came in a big ship, in which they lived all the time, and went out in boats to kill whales. When they speared one, a man would pick it up and put it on the ship.

Giant white men who speared whales. They cooked the meat in an enormous iron pot and drank the oil.

Drawing by Santo Blanco.

They cooked the whale meat in an enormous iron pot, ate it and drank the oil. They did not drink mezcal, but smoked lots of tobacco. This was in the time of the Antigua Seris, before the Yoris came. They wore hats so big it took twelve men to lift them, and had a liquor of their own. They would not sell this liquor—they drank it themselves. It is said they were very happy when they were drinking, and they sang this when they were drunk.

SONG OF THE GIANTS:

The Mother Carey's chicken cannot eat.
The wind blows and the waves are rough.

For two days it did not rain
No sardines appeared
And the little cock could not eat.

This seemed to be all about Mother Carey's chicken, and not a word about the giants.

"The sea," explained Santo Blanco, "drives the sardines to the surface. That is why the little cock could not eat."

He paused and thought a while, but could not bring himself to go on.

"This song," he said, "was sung by an old man, long ago."

THE BABY SHARK:

The baby shark came close to shore.
He was dying.
The Seris cooked him
But the meat was not good.
The coyote ate him.

"The baby coyote smelled him," went on Santo Blanco reminiscently, "but he would not eat him."

There was a long silence then, and at last he began to sing:

THE WHALE SONG:

1. The sea was very red.
   The giants looked into the water
   And on the bottom they could see
   All the whales.

"On the west side of Tiburon, on the beach," observed Santo Blanco, "there are the remains of a spear used by these giants. When the Seris see it on the shore as they pass, they look in wonder and say: *'Soo yeh-eh'*—this is a— But they cannot find any name for it, it is so big. This giant is so big the bees make their nests in his mouth. When he opens it, the honey drips out. When he smokes his great pipe the bees fly away—and there is so much smoke they stay away for eight days."

These details were just put in to kill time and keep from telling us what we wanted. *All* Seri giants have hats so big it takes twelve or more men to lift them, and the bees or wasps or scorpions always make nests in their mouths or hair. So we waited and at last he said:

"The giant's front teeth were white, but all his back teeth were made of gold."

They must have been very modern giants, to have gold inlays in their molars, but Santo Blanco was not through.

"They wore rings of gold in their ears," he went on, "and a large one in their noses."

After all, these must have been real sailor-men who came to Tiburon so long ago, since old sailors always wear earrings, and Santo Blanco was so heartened by our joy over this discovery that he went ahead with the song.

2. Far off on the sea a whale spouts.
   The giants follow him in their boat.
   The whale goes deep to the bottom.
   They spear him in the head
   And the sea is red with blood.

"These Ancients sang a song. This is the song:

    3. The sea is calm. The whale is happy.
        I follow him as he runs
        On top of the water—happy.
        Soon I will be happy.
        I will kill him.

"This is the end of the Giant Song."

Santo Blanco paused as he made his announcement. Then he added:

"There is another verse to this Song of the Giants, but I have forgotten it. If I talk to God tonight I can remember it."

Here it was again, this strange inability to remember the last verse of a song, and like a flash the reason came to me. In the summer-time—when my Navajo medicine man was not supposed to tell snake and lightning stories—he would give me three parts of a song or story and conveniently forget the fourth. As long as he sang only a part of the song he would not incur the anger of the gods, but the fourth and last verse would finish it and so make his breach complete. He was really doing me a favor to talk about the lightning at all—and so it was with Santo Blanco and his giants.

Of all the Indians I have known he was the least swayed by superstitious fears, and he had some good reason for not telling about these giants. Either fear of the gods held him back or the subject was taboo among his people. He would never finish these songs. But the White Giants were undoubtedly whalers, magnified to the stature of giants by the passage of centuries, their every act exaggerated in the telling until it only suggested the truth.

"How large was the ship of these giants?" I asked; and Santo Blanco was glad to change the subject.

"It was so big that four whales would not fill it. The men sat in front and behind, but not in the middle of the boat."

I had visions of the caravels of ancient days in which Columbus discovered America—with the waist very low and the bow and stern very high, like the Chinese junks of today. But it turned out to be another kind.

"How long ago was it that they came?"

"Long after Ahnt ah ko'-mah, the Wise Man. First of all into the world came the Wise Woman. Then came her man. Then Ahnt ah ko'-mah. Then Ahnt Kai'. Afterwards came these giants. They came only once, and the Seris were afraid of them. All except the Old Wise Woman, who talked with them. They took four families of Seris away with them, who were all afraid to go. The Giants promised to bring them back when they returned; but they never came back.

"The Giants stayed at Tiburon a year and four months, cooking their whale-meat [trying out the oil]. Their paddles were so big that each stroke would push them half a league [sweeps]. They did not row backwards—they paddled forward. They had no sails on their small boats. Two men paddled—one on each side.

"There were many men and one woman in the ship, and they told the Ancient Seris there were many more like them in their country. They lived in big houses, by the sea. These Giants took the old man who sings this song [composed it] to their ship and told him about their home. They said that in their country

Woman From Afar, the wife of the Giant Whaler. She was whiter than the men and had red hair, which she wore in big braids down her back. Her carrying-basket was so large it held two whales, and she has a third in her hand.

Drawing by Santo Blanco.

they hunted a deer so big that only a Giant could kill one. The Captain told the Old Wise Woman its name was Ahp kah′ roh [probably an elk].

"They had bows and arrows—the arrows as big around as the circle of my fingers [six inches]. No, they had no shields. The hide of these Giants was so thick that no Seri arrow would **penetrate it.**

Ahn tay hai-tem, Brother of the Giant Whaler. He wore boots on the ship, but when he hunted deer on the mainland he wore sandals. All the weapons they had were bows and arrows and spears.

Drawing by Santo Blanco.

"The Giant Woman was the wife of the Captain. She was whiter than the men and had red hair. She had big braids down her back. She was dressed in thick clothes, and a big cloak or mantle went over her back. Her carrying-basket was so big, they could cut a whale in two and she would put one-half in her basket.

"The story says their shoes were very big and wide, but when they went hunting they took off these shoes and wore sandals. They hunted on the mainland— they would have turned the Island over if they had hunted there. They always slept in their boat and had no camp on shore. They went hunting very early in the morning. All the weapons they had were bows and arrows and spears. But that was long ago and the Seris do not know any more."

After telling this brief tale Santo Blanco seemed very anxious to go, so I paid him his peso and a half and went ahead with my packing. But he had not finished with me yet. Borrowing a sheaf of paper he hurried back home, where he painted so many pictures of Came From Afar Man, his wife, his giant brother and his boat, that the last of my doubts was dispelled.

Sometime, long ago—when men still fought with bows and arrows, but after the beginning of the whaling industry—his people had seen a whaler. Observing the crew cooking the blubber, they had taken it for granted that they ate it; but the length of their stay, a year and four months, gives evidence that they were trying out the oil. A whole shipload! And when they had filled all their casks and barrels, they took four families of the Indians and departed.

Here was a subject on which a man could spend a lifetime of research—the landing on the west coast of Mexico of blue-eyed wanderers, with yellow hair—

but it was evident that Santo Blanco had told us all he intended to, and the low clouds were heavy with rain. We struck the big tent, loaded our plunder on the cars and prepared to leave at dawn. But as I sat by the fire that evening and talked about the Giants with Angelito Coronado, he proved what I had surmised from the start. These whalers were Norwegians.

For thirty years I had been hearing from the Mexicans about the blue-eyed white people who had sailed up the Mayo River and founded the Mayo nation. The Mayos are good Indians—the best on the West Coast —and even the warlike Yaquis could never conquer them. Cajeme, the great war chief of the Yaquis, was a blue-eyed, yellow-haired Mayo; and when he led them to victory he made every man pay him tribute. He had a genius for military strategy that no black Yaqui could equal, and he was proud of his Yori blood.

After I had expressed my admiration for these Indians and my intention of making them a visit, Angelito laughed and said:

"I am a Mayo—*puro!*"

Right in my camp, all the time I had been investigating the Seris, I had had a lineal descendant of the sea-roving Vikings who had sailed up the Mayo River. But Angelito, like his people, had been Mexicanized until the memory of his bold ancestors had vanished. He knew, or would tell, nothing; and the following year, when I went to the Mayo River, I had very little success in getting the story of their coming. But, from a white man I met who had married into the tribe, I learned the details of their ancient wedding ceremony; and three features of it were identical with the old Norwegian rites.

The girl's father and mother had kissed his hand

and her hand and he had to drink with all comers. A great feast had been given, and at its close the Head Chief had filled a glass full of cognac and told him to drink it all—until he did that he was not married. As a final rite, pretty girls had strewn flowers before them, and he and his bride had had to walk over them, crushing them underfoot.

There can be very little doubt that Santo Blanco's White Giants were of the same blood as these visitors to the Mayos; and both may have dated back to the Vikings, when the vessels of those adventurous Norsemen were faring to the ends of the earth.

We know from King Alfred's account of Othere's voyage to the White Sea that the Norwegians were expert whalers a thousand years ago; and, since these Mexican giants had no firearms, they probably came before Columbus. Came From Afar Man, with his four families of Seris, must have perished on the long voyage home. But on Tiburon his fame still endures, though soon enough it will be forgotten.

The Seris are dying off rapidly but, as long as Santo Blanco lives, the glories of the old days will be sung. Through his stories and songs, we had gone back for a moment to a time when there were giants in the land —giants and gods, flying around through the night and warning him not to talk too much. No doubt it was the fear of them which had shut him up, and kept him from finishing his songs.

He was back again for breakfast, filling up on a last feast of rice before we went away. Then, deprecatingly, he asked for our empty oil-tins, if we were not going to use them any more. There was also a pile of wood, which would save his wife and daughters a long

journey into the monte; and any food that Angelito
did not want, he would be glad to have that, too.

They came then, Loreta Lupe and her eight smiling
daughters and carried away all they could; but as we
drove past the Lodge they ran out to meet us, with
more drawings in their hands. Pictures of women with
long poles, gathering fruit from the giant cactus;
delicate face paintings made by all but the youngest;

A woman being bitten by a rattlesnake while gathering
cactus-pears.

Drawing by Lupita Blanco.

and canoes, with sea turtles being speared. We bought them all, at twenty centavos apiece, and drove off, leaving them happy.

The little man of whom it had been said that he thought of nothing but money, had given us more than all the rest; and as he looked after us, smiling, I thought how easy it had been to change him into a friend. He lives in a world where the gods still rule, looking down from high Tiburon; and for a few Mexican pesos he had taken us behind the veil, as far as a white man can go.

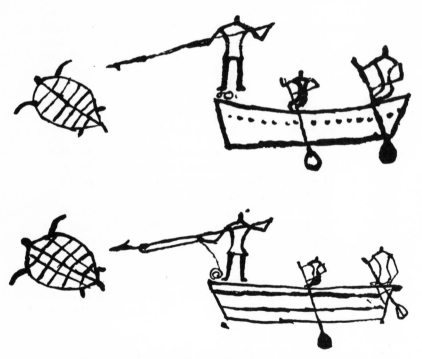

Spearing turtles—Santo Blanco's last picture.

APPENDIX

Seri Deities

1. He Who Rules Earth And Sky (Ahnt ahs' po-mee'-kay) "God." Corresponding to the Zeus of the Greeks. A very ugly-looking god, living in Heaven where he reigns over the spirits of the dead for eight days. He then comes to earth for eight days, to bring back the souls of those who have died.

2. His Wife. A very white woman (the Greek Juno).

3. I Am Very Wise (Say-say ai-khai ai'-pay). A friendly god. He lives 32 months on earth and then returns to Heaven. He dwells in the Holy Cave on Tiburon Island, and the men and boys make sacrifices to him.

4. His Wife (Say-say ai-khai ai'-pay—Mahm-m). Spoken of as Mahm-m—woman. The goddess of women.

5. Ahnt Kai'. Goddess of women and children, to whom they make their sacrifices. Daughter of First Woman by the sun. (The Athene of the Greeks, Kwan Yin of the Buddhists. Est-san ad'lehi of the Navajos.) She dwells in a white house above the highest peak of Tiburon and flies around at night. The only god who can order the Fish Dance. Like Pallas Athene she has no relations with men.

6. Ahnt ahs pok'. Daughter of Ahnt Kai'. A little girl, two feet high, to whom the Seri girls pray and offer sacrifices of dew, in white shells. She lives with her mother on Tiburon.

7. The Wind God (Aeolus of the Greeks). He lives in a cave beneath the sea and sends forth good and bad winds.

8. First Woman (Koo-mah′mm hahs-ay′ tahm). Painted Woman—Beautiful Woman. Mother of Ahnt Kai′, and the Seris.

9. First Man. He lives with He Who Rules The Sky, in Heaven, and never dies.

10. Daughter Of The Gods (Sahk Kays′ Es Yo Sees′ Kak Aht), Daughter of First Woman and the Sun. Goddess of young girls.

11. Flying Around In The Night (Ahn-tee-ehp′ Kwee-mee′-kay). He lives in the Holy Cave on top of Tiburon and dominates during the hot weather. To him the Seri men make offerings of *pitahayas* and cactus fruits.

12. Wants A Flower (Ahn-tee-up′). His son. He rules in the cold weather. A man-god who lives in the center of Tiburon and makes the flowers grow.

13. Flying Around In The Sky (Kwee-kee′ kai es-scop′-oh). The Old Wise Woman.

14. After Four Days The Seris Will Die (Kwin-kay-hai′ so-hay tal hoz′). An evil man-god, who calls people to their death.

15. The Sun (the Greek Apollo).

16. The Moon. His Wife (the Greek Diana).

17. Father Sky.

18. Mother Earth. His Wife (the Greek Gaea).

19. Ahnt ah zu′-mah. A man-god who came down from Heaven and stayed on earth a month. A small white man with yellow hair; dressed in a black robe, like a priest. He taught the Seris to wear Ahnt-ah zu′-mah crowns on ceremonial occasions.

20. Man Who Built Fires (Ahnt ah ko′-mah). A culture-hero, like Hiawatha and the Star Child. A tall

white man with a long, white beard. He came from the west in a boat and taught the Seris how to build fires and how to live.

21. The Spirit of the Holy Cave. A source of magical power.

22. The House Gods (Eh-ek ahk-mee'-ket). Two-legged figurine. (Eh-ow kmee'-kee et quop.) One-legged figurine.

Folio of Modern Photographs
of the
Seri Indians
in and around
Kino Bay, Sonora, Mexico

-o-

Photographs supplied by Arizona
State Museum, Tucson, Ariz., with
photographer as indicated. Courtesy
Dr. Raymond H. Thompson,
Director, Arizona State Museum

(Most of these are posed pictures
taken as the caption indicates)

-o-

Photographs by Robert B. McCoy
were all taken in February 1971.

Courtesy Arizona State Museum.   Photo: James W. Manson, 1955.

THE SERI INDIANS ARE A HANDSOME PEOPLE.

Courtesy Arizona State Museum.   Photo: James W. Manson, 1957.

AN ATTRACTIVE SERI WOMAN.

Courtesy Arizona State Museum.   Photo: James W. Manson, n.d.

A SERI ELDER.

Courtesy Arizona State Museum.   Photo: James W. Manson, 1957.

A SERI MATRIARCH.

Courtesy Arizona State Museum.

Photo: James W. Manson, n.d.

SERI BOY MEETS SERI GIRL.

271

Courtesy Arizona State Museum.

THE UPCOMING GENERATION OF SERI BOYS.

Photo: Helga Teiwes, n.d.

Courtesy Arizona State Museum.   Photo: C.E. Ronstadt, n.d.

SHY AND WORRIED.

Courtesy Arizona State Museum.   Photo: James W. Manson, 1963.

FIXING A MEAL WITH MODERN EQUIPMENT.

274

Photo: James W. Manson, 1960.

SERI FAMILY SCENE.

Courtesy Arizona State Museum.

Photo: James W. Manson, 1961.

BOY AND GIRL

Courtesy Arizona State Museum.

Courtesy Arizona State Museum.   Photo: James W. Manson, 1963.

THE SERIS EAT TORTILLAS, TOO.

Courtesy, Arizona State Museum.   Photo: Gwyneth Harrington, n.d.

NOT VANITY; A CEREMONIAL TASK.

Photo: Helga Teiwes, n.d.

WITH APOLOGIES TO ARMOUR & CO.: THE DOG KIDS LOVE TO BITE. NOTE, AMONG OTHER THINGS, THE IRONWOOD CARVING IN PRODUCTION.

Photo: James W. Manson, n.d.

HOME IS WHERE YOU MAKE IT.

Courtesy, Arizona State Museum.

280

FISH SHED, OLD KINO BAY VILLAGE.

Photo: Robert B. McCoy, 1971.

Photo: Robert B. McCoy, 1971.

NOT INDIANS. MEXICAN MUCHACHAS (?) MUCHACHOS (?) ON THE BEACH AT OLD KINO BAY VILLAGE.

KINO BAY FISHING BOATS; ISLA ALCATRAZ IN THE BACKGROUND.

Photo: Robert B. McCoy, 1971.

Photo: Robert B. McCoy, 1971.

SCENE ON KINO BAY BEACH.

284

Photo: Robert B. McCoy, 1971.

CATHOLIC CHURCH AT OLD KINO BAY VILLAGE.

Photo: Robert B. McCoy, 1971.

MAIN STREET, OLD KINO BAY VILLAGE. REFRESHMENTS AVAILABLE AT THE TECATE BAR.

Photo: Robert B. McCoy, 1971.

MAIN STREET'S MAIN INTERSECTION, OLD KINO BAY VILLAGE.

THE LONG AVENIDA INTO NEW KINO BAY VILLAGE. NOTE TIBURON ISLAND AT LEFT, FAR, FAR BACK—GROUND.

Photo: Robert B. McCoy, 1971.

288

Photo: Robert B. McCoy, 1971.

MOTEL KINO BAY.

MOTEL KINO BAY HAS A NICE TRAILER PARK.

Photo: Robert B. McCoy, 1971.

SHRINES TO OUR LADY OF GUADALUPE OVERLOOK NEW KINO BAY VILLAGE.

Photo: Robert B. McCoy, 1971.

BUS SERVICE DOWNTOWN NEW KINO BAY VILLAGE TO HERMOSILLO AND BACK.

Photo: Robert B. McCoy, 1971.

Photo: Robert B. McCoy, 1971.

PATIO OF A LUXURY HOME ON THE AVENIDA, NEW KINO BAY VILLAGE.

Photo: Robert B. McCoy, 1971.

BEACHSIDE VIEW OF COLORFUL MOTEL SANTA GAMMA.

294

Photo: Robert B. McCoy, 1971.

TYPICAL LUXURY HOME (THERE ARE MANY) ON THE AVENIDA, NEW KINO BAY VILLAGE.

Photo: Robert B. McCoy, 1971.

ANOTHER LUXURY HOME ON THE BEACH, NEW KINO BAY VILLAGE.

296

A SERI IRONWOOD CARVING OF A SHARK.

Photo: Robert B. McCoy, 1971.

A SERI IRONWOOD CARVING OF A FISH.

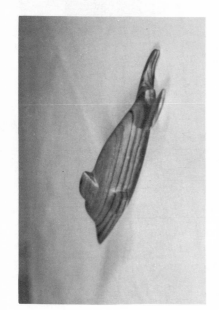

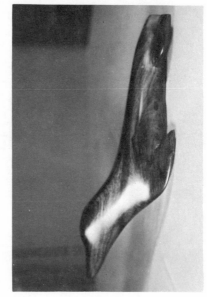

Photos: Robert B. McCoy, 1971.

SERI IRONWOOD CARVINGS; A SHARK, A QUAIL AND A SEAL.

Photo: Robert B. McCoy, 1971.

LA LOMA BLANCA RESTAURANT AT POSADA DEL MAR.

Photo: Robert B. McCoy, 1971.

GARDENS AND FRONT ENTRANCE TO POSADA DEL MAR. ALL VEGETATION IS STILL YOUNG; MOTEL ONLY OPENED FOR BUSINESS IN MARCH 1970.

301

Photo: Robert B. McCoy, 1971.

FORMAL GARDENS, POSADA DEL MAR. PALM TREES ARE STILL YOUNG AND TENDER.

Photo: Robert B. McCoy, 1971.

VIEW FROM THE BALCONY OF POSADA DEL MAR; ISLA ALCATRAZ IN THE BAY.

Photo: Robert B. McCoy, 1971.

POSADA DEL MAR PROVIDES A HANDSOME POOL FOR GUESTS TOO TIMID TO SWIM IN THE DELIGHTFUL GULF OF CALIFORNIA HALF A BLOCK DISTANT.

Photo: Robert B. McCoy, 1971.

SERGIO GONZALES IN FRONT OF LA LOMA BLANCA RESTAURANTE. OUR EXCELLENT ENGLISH–SPEAKING GUIDE.

Photo: Robert B. McCoy, 1971.

PARTNER JOHN STRACHAN AND FRIEND EDWARD RUDA LOAFING IT UP ON THE TERRACE.

LONG VIEW OF ENTRANCE TO POSADA DEL MAR. LA LOMA BLANCA RESTAURANTE IS AT RIGHT.

Photo: Robert B. McCoy, 1971.